BATTERIES NOT INCLUDED
What to do when life happens!!!

"For we are his workmanship, created in Christ Jesus unto good works, which God hath before ordained that we should walk in them"

LOGAN FERGUSON

Copyright © 2015 by Logan Ferguson

Batteries Not Included
What to do when life happens!!!

by Logan Ferguson

Printed in the United States of America.

ISBN 9781498436168

All rights reserved solely by the author. The author guarantees all contents are original and do not infringe upon the legal rights of any other person or work. No part of this book may be reproduced in any form without the permission of the author. The views expressed in this book are not necessarily those of the publisher.

Unless otherwise indicated, Scripture quotations taken from the New International Version (NIV). Copyright © 1973, 1978, 1984, 2011 by Biblica, Inc.™. Used by permission. All rights reserved.

www.xulonpress.com

Life happens fast and circumstances arise.
So what do I do when my faith is tested?
How Do I handle life?
What do I do when I question God?
I don't have the answers?!?!
I wish this came with batteries!
Don't get trapped by life! Live to the fullest! Live life like it depends on God…..because it DOES!!!

Contents

~

Identity Crisis 11
    Who am I; really? I want to be known as somebody.
    I want to be known for something in this life. People
    who struggle with their identity will settle for less
    than God has for them and they will never embrace
    Christ and His work in them. I need batteries!

Shaken Faith 23
    I trusted God with my life and things haven't turned
    out like I thought they should. I have questioned
    God and now I don't even know where to turn. Why
    has God seemed to abandon me? I need batteries!

Adversity: Sometimes Life Is Too Much 29
    I'm trying. I'm doing the right things in this
    Christian life. It just seems that bad luck follows me.
    Every time I turn around I find myself in an adverse
    situation. I need batteries!

Surrender. 40
    I thought I gave my life over to God?!? What more
    does God want or expect from me? I try filing spots
    in my life with Godly activity. But He keeps telling
    me to let go of the plow. What does that mean? I
    need batteries!

Worship: Opening Your Heart, Head, and Hands ..47
   I just can't get into it! Maybe I don't understand the true concept behind "worship"? I've given God my heart; so what else does He expect of me? I need batteries!

Influence 53
   Influence is either positive or negative. There's no middle ground. How do I reach the next level and take people with me? I need batteries!

Forgiveness: Everyone Needs It (Yes You) 58
   Before you can forgive others you must be able to forgive yourself. Forgiveness starts in your heart. I'm tired of living in agony over the decisions I've made in life. I need batteries!

Loving Others: Sounds Simple, But It's Hard ...66
   Loving the unlovable is one of the hardest things that Jesus asked/commanded us to do. It's easy to love the people we are "supposed" to love – family, friends, etc. So how do I love people that I don't even like? I need batteries!

Jesus Extra 76
   The work of the Holy Spirit is a unique thing. It's hard to grasp and comprehend. However; there is a difference between having the Holy Spirit in you than being full of the Holy Spirit. Wait!!! What?!?! I need batteries!

Fight From Where God Told You 85
   The concept of "pick your battles" is irrelevant in today's society. Although you may not be able to pick most of your battles in life, you can pick from where you fight from. Don't run from your circumstances; run to the battle lines that God has for you. I need batteries!

Contents

Winning The War 104
    Yes! You are outnumbered in life. You cannot and will not win!!! But God can win through you. And yes…you will need batteries!

Finish Strong. 115
    Everybody messes up in life and everyone makes mistakes. But it's not about the mistakes you've made; it's about how you finish. I need a chance at a major comeback in life. I need batteries!

There's Hope: An Encouraging Word
From The Author. 125

About The Author 127

Introduction

The title for the book came to life a long time ago when I was in a department store shopping for some materials for an upcoming mission trip. After several hours and two baskets full of items, I was standing in a very long checkout line (patience) and I was looking at one of my items reading a little bit about it when I noticed in small letters that it said "Batteries Not Included". Great! And wouldn't you know it; there wasn't a battery section anywhere close to me. And I was determined that I wasn't going to drag two buggies back across this busy store and lose my place in line.

It was in that moment that God spoke to me and said, "Logan, there are many people and Christians who live defeated lives because they've never picked up the batteries that I've placed in their lives for them to use". Well, I just kind of ignored that still small voice and went on about my business, stopping at a dollar store to pick up my batteries. However, God wouldn't leave me alone about it. So I turned this concept into a series that became an in-depth Bible

Batteries Not Included

study. Then God gave me a greater vision; write a book. What? Write a book? God, you must not know where I went to school at.

After seeking advice; because that's what you just do when God speaks to you because you really don't believe Him (You know I'm right. At least I admit it), someone close to me said, and I quote, "Logan you can't write a book, but God can write it through you". Needless to say, but I needed batteries.

My prayer for you as you read through this book and you study the stories behind each situation is that God will mold you and show you that He is the One with unlimited batteries…and His batteries never run out of juice. They do not need to be recharged or recycled because He is the power source behind every situation that you will ever face.

So if you need batteries; buckle up and let's do this together.

Chapter 1
Identity Crisis

Who am I?

We all have an identity crisis. Every single one of us have this problem. We may not like to admit it, but we do. We all go through seasons in life where we struggle with who we are and what we've become. What we have to establish first is the meaning to the word "identity". I asked several anonymous people to define for me the word "identity". Some of the responses were comical while others were rather serious. Someone even told me, "my driver's license". Well, on one sense they were right, but when it relates to who we are this person was completely wrong.

Webster defined the word identity as, "who or what a person is".[1]

---

[1] Webster's Dictionary & Thesaurus. Identity. Polskabook. Poland. 2006. 185.

Batteries Not Included

Jeff Foxworthy has always been a funny guy. I've always like him. Foxworthy became huge when he started identifying who or what a redneck really is. How do you know if you're really a redneck? His infamous line "you might be a redneck if.........." will forever stick in our minds as some of the greatest ways to identify a redneck. Now we must understand that the term "redneck" is just a play on words. My apologies if I just ruined everything your parents taught you.

For the sake of fun, and because I've been guilty myself of some of these, I picked out a few of my favorite redneck lines from the great Jeff Foxworthy. You might be a redneck if..........You cut your grass and find a car. You might be a redneck if..........You hit a deer with your car; on purpose. You might be a redneck if..........You've ever stolen toilet paper. You might be a redneck if..........People hear your car before they see it. You might be a redneck if.......... Your step-dad is also your uncle. You might be a redneck if..........You record wrestling.

It's just a fact that people want to be identified with something; even if it is a redneck......or even something really bad. We all want an identity. We want to be known as the person who _____. When we can identify with something it makes us feel like we belong. If you've given your life to Christ you do belong. You belong to God. You don't have to try fitting into clicks or groups. Your identity is in Christ – not what someone says about you, not what someone thinks about you. It's about Christ. That's it!

Ephesians 2:10 gives us a beautiful picture of God and how He ensures us that we take on the image of Christ. And this verse is the driving point behind this book. Read carefully what it says. *"For we are his workmanship, created in Christ Jesus unto good works, which God hath before ordained that we should walk in them"* (King James Version).

I am a work of art

"For we are his *workmanship*". Workmanship is a key word here. Some versions say "we are his *masterpiece*". And in the Greek it uses the word "masterpiece". Wait a minute. You are telling me that I am God's masterpiece? Yes! That's not only what I'm telling you, but it's what God is telling you.

When you are a *masterpiece,* you are the absolute greatest thing ever created. All artists have what they would call their greatest piece of work. All song writers have what they call their greatest piece of work. They cherish it and they love it. That's what we are to God. He cherishes us and He loves us because we are His greatest piece of work.

So if we are God's "masterpiece" then we are His greatest work, right? There's nothing more special in God's eyes than you!!! Now let me show you something cool. This will prove that you are special to God and that you are His greatest piece of work. In the progression of the creation account in Genesis chapter one, everything that God created He said was *good*. The light was good, the dry ground was good, the vegetation was good, and the creation of the animals was good. When God saw all that He created He said it was *good*.

Up to this point in the creation story everything that God made was good. However, God is going to get real personal now because He is about to make man (you and me) in His very image. When God does this it goes beyond being good. So check this out......

"So God created man in his own image, in the image of God he created him; male and female he created them. God blessed them and said to them, "Be fruitful and increase in number; fill the earth and subdue it. Rule over the fish of the sea and the birds of the air and over every living creature that moves on the ground". Then God said, "I give you every seed-bearing plant on the face of the whole earth and every tree that has fruit with seed in it. They will be yours for food. And to all the beasts of the earth and all the birds of the air and all the creatures that move on the ground – everything that has the breath of life in it – I give every green plant for food". And it was so. God saw all that he had made, and it was very good". Genesis 1:27-31

Everything was "good" until God created the first human being. That's when God said it was "very good". The reason God said "very good" is because we are His masterpiece, making us His greatest work. Therefore, our identity is found in God through Christ;

Identity Crisis

and that identity never changes. When God looks at you He sees you through His Son Jesus.

In the movie *The Hanging Tree* starring Gary Cooper (1959 western), Gary Cooper plays a doctor that moved into a mining community in Montana. There was a young man who got shot and was dying. But the doctor removed the bullet and saved his life. So the young man was willing to do anything as payment. So the doctor says, "I need an assistant". The young man then asks, "for how long"? In which the doctor has the best line ever; "for the rest of your life because if I haven't of saved you that's how long you would have been dead".[2]

"For the rest of your life". I just love that because that puts a major emphasis on who we are. Our identity states who we are and God states that we are His for the rest of our lives all the way into eternity. Your identity is not your driver's license; That's just a picture. Your identity is not your social security number; That's just how the government keeps up with you. Your identity is not your school ID. You get the point. Your real identity is found in Christ. If you have surrendered your life to Christ that's the identity that you take on.

In Galatians chapter two verse twenty the Apostle Paul gives us a beautiful picture of who we are through Christ. Paul understood this and he shared with us some powerful words when he said *"I am*

---

[2] Evan, Tony. Tony Evan's Book of Illustrations. Moody Publishers. Chicago. 2009. 141.

crucified with Christ: nevertheless I live; yet not I, but Christ liveth in me" (King James Version).

You want to know what Paul is saying? "You look at me and you see Paul. God looks at me and sees His Son". That's what it's about. It's about Jesus being seen in you. Yes, people will look at you and see the mistakes you have made and see you for who you are NOT. Understand this, it's about who you know you really are. Every day when you wake up you need to steal the words of the Apostle Paul and say to yourself, "I have been crucified with Christ". When you give your life to Christ you have taken on a new identity. It's not what or who people see that matters; it's who God sees that matters. So let me ask you; when God looks at you, who does He see?

Have you ever been so consumed by life's circumstances that you lost your identity? You forgot who you were? Sometimes our problems swallow up our identity. But you are not to be known by your problems because it doesn't matter what people say about you. If you say that you are a Christian then your identity is found in Christ. Don't ever let someone tell you who you are based on your circumstances. Your identity is in Christ. So when God looks at you He doesn't look at how jacked up you may be, He sees the person that His Son died for.

New identity equals freedom

When I was in the eighth grade I had to walk home from school because both of my parents worked until after five. There was a neighborhood that I walked

Identity Crisis

through so that I wouldn't have to walk along the highway. There was this particular house that had a huge dog in the front yard and he was chained to a tree. I have no idea what type of dog he was, but I distinctly remember that he wanted to kill me every afternoon when I walked by the house. He had that chain stretched to the very end in an attempt to bite my head off. His bark was ferocious. With everything inside of me, I'm telling you that he wanted me for an afternoon snack. But there was this one day in particular that as I approached the yard I noticed that the dog was off

his chain. Needless to say, but me and the Lord established a very intimate relationship at that point. As walked briskly past the dog I also noticed that as he stood there barking and still wanting to kill me that he didn't go past where the chain would have usually stopped him.

The dog was free and didn't even know it because he had spent his entire life chained up. I wander how many of us live our lives under the yoke of slavery and never realize that the chains are gone and we are free? When we take on the identity of Christ we take on a new found freedom. The chains are gone. You've been set free.

> *"So you are no longer a slave, but a son; and since you are a son, God has made you also an heir"*. Galatians 4:7

Some of us are living our lives as slaves. We are slaves to something. It may be that secret sin that you

Batteries Not Included

have hidden deep in your life that no one else knows about. You may be a slave to a relationship. You may even be a slave to your work or even the standard that has been placed on you. If you are reading this and you are a working professional; you may be a slave to your job and you are sacrificing your family in the process. Therefore that makes you feel trapped – like you can't get out. I know what you are going through. I have been a slave to every one of those. If you are a parent, let your kid be a kid and do kid stuff. You may not realize it, but you have them enslaved.

Let me ask you this question to think about; Have you ever been locked in a room; either by accident or on purpose? How did it make you feel? Reflect on that for a few moments.

When I was a little boy, about nine years old, we attended a little country church. The building was to say the least, raggedy. It was an old block building and it had a unique smell. Doors didn't open and close properly; and the locks on the bathroom doors malfunctioned quite a bit. One Sunday morning during the preaching service my bladder attacked me. I had to pee so dang bad and I couldn't hold it any longer. Most of the time my parents wouldn't dare let me get up during church. But this one time my dad had mercy on me and allowed me to go to the bathroom. The bathroom was located directly behind the choir loft. My dad gave me one instruction: Do Not lock the bathroom door. Well, I was a big boy and I knew how to work the lock…..or so I thought. After relieving my bladder of the excruciating pain I couldn't get the door to unlock. So I instantly panicked. Let me pause to say this: I honestly thought I would spend the rest of my life in the bathroom of an old creepy church. I knew within that moment that no one would come to save me. Back to the story; so I panicked and began hitting and kicking the bathroom door while screaming like a little girl in the process. Little did I know, but the entire church heard what was going on. So my dad came to the bathroom door and talked me through unlocking it. I wish I could tell you that I had a wonderful Sunday afternoon…….but I would be lying.

So let's break this down: What is a slave? *Slave* = "person owned by another". What is a son? A *son* is a direct descendent. What is an heir? *Heir* = "one who inherits or is entitled to something". Through Christ we go from slave to son to heir. What are we? So if we are no longer a slave, but a son – which in turn makes us an heir; in Christ, what are we entitled to? It's not that God owes us something, but that He has promised us something. And because He has promised us something that means we are entitled to it, right?

What do I receive?

What we receive through this entitlement here on earth is not the promise of a pain free life. However, we are promised that we don't have to live as slaves to our sin or live in bondage because of someone else. The price for our freedom has been paid for. So don't let the ferocious dog or the bathroom lock, or anything else hinder you from living a life of freedom.

The ultimate entitlement that we will receive we will receive it when we get to Heaven. We will then become co-heirs with Christ.

"For you did not receive a spirit that makes you a slave again to fear, but you received the Spirit of sonship. And by him we cry "Abba Father". The Spirit himself testifies with our spirit that we are God's children. Now if we are children, then we are heirs – heirs of God and co-heirs with Christ". Romans 8:15-17a

Notice in the scripture some key words of emphasis like "slave, sonship, and heir". When you become a child of God, that's what your identity becomes. You're not a slave anymore because Jesus set you free. No slave has ever called their master or boss "Father". But that's what God is. He's our Father.

One of the definitions for the word "father" is "protector". Guess what? That's exactly what God does. Not only does He protect us but He protects our identity. When He looks at you He sees His Son, His heir, the one who will inherit all that He has for you. You are His child making you His heir and Him your Father and Protector.

When we are born we are slaves because we are sinners. We can't help it because it's just what we are born into. Here's the beautiful thing about God; even while we were sinners Christ died for us (Romans chapter five verse six). Everyone who receives Jesus and believes in Him becomes a child of God. Now that you can call God your Father you are His son, making you an heir.

Identity Crisis

Where do you want your identity to be? Is your identity found in what you are trapped in? Or is your identity in Christ? Your identity is up to you. You're the only person who can change your condition.

Time of reflection

* Who are you, really? Do you have an identity crisis today?
* What is it that you are struggling to be identified with? Is it a click or a group, a fad or a fashion, or is it Christ Himself?
* What lie about yourself have you allowed yourself to buy into? You are God's greatest piece of work. Don't let someone else control your identity.
* What are you consumed by right now?
* Remember; freedom is found in Christ. Reflect on that for a few moments.
* Whatever it is that you are locked in right now, let the Father guide you through unlocking that part of your life so that you can experience freedom. If you don't, you will wake up 50 years from now and wonder what happened.
* Take a few moments and think and pray about what you're going to receive with this freedom in Christ.

Prayer for Batteries

Lord, help me to understand who I am in You! Please, keep from seeking after labels. I am who I am because You made me and molded me in Your very image. I know that through Christ I am no longer a slave but a son and also an heir. Help me to hold on to the promises You have given me. I am Yours!

Chapter 2
Shaken Faith

I got this faith thing!

One of the easiest things to say to people when they are struggling is to "just have faith". I'm going to be honest with you; sometimes that's the last thing I want to hear when I'm struggling through an issue. Now let me tell you why; because most of the people who say that stuff to you, they don't even believe it themselves when they are struggling. So don't tell me something that you have trouble believing yourself. Then on top of that we hear people say something ridiculous like, "maybe God is punishing you for something". Then I'm thinking, "Maybe I should punch you now and let some of this stress out".

That's all in good fun, but on a serious note: What do we do when our faith has been shaken? Because here's the kicker: Faith is the glue that holds our Christian life together. Without faith, what do we really have? Faith is a way of life. Without faith all we

Batteries Not Included

have is a movement and not a lifestyle. Movements don't last, but a lifestyle does.

Let me ask you: How come when life is going great, God is good all the time? Then, when life hits that valley or bump in the road all of a sudden we begin to question God? Our faith all of a sudden is shaken. You see, it's easy to tell other people to have faith when their life is haywire and yours is hunky-dory. What happens when that is reversed? What happens when you suddenly become the one questioning God and asking Him the "why" questions?

Let's set it up like this: What are some things or people that we have faith in? For the sake of this activity and for your mind to be jostled a moment, let's remove God from the faith equation. The reason is because God is always the first response to this question. Now we can put the pieces together. So again I'm asking you; What are some things or people that we have faith in? Maybe it's the lights, your car, the water facet, your athletic ability, your parents, your grand-parents, your job, your income, or maybe even your pastor? What is it that makes that faith strong? What does that ability, power source, or person possess that causes you to put your entire stock into it or them?

Jesus teaches us about a man who was the greatest ever born of a woman. I'm not making this up; these words are in red in your Bible meaning they came from the very lips of our Savior. On a side note: I don't believe that Jesus said this about the man because they were cousins. I believe Jesus was giving us an honest assessment about the guy. Look at what Jesus said…..

"I tell you the truth: Among those born of women there has not risen anyone greater than John the Baptist" Matthew 11:11a

I can't emphasize this enough, but did you notice what Jesus said about John the Baptist? Read the middle part of that verse again and think about what an honor it would be to have the Savior of the world say that about a human being. So after reading and rereading this verse, what would you say about the faith of John the Baptist?

John the Baptist was the greatest man born of a woman. That's not an opinion or speculation. That's a fact because that comes from the mouth of God Himself. Jesus said it so you know it's the truth. John the Baptist was preaching about Jesus before Jesus even came on the scene. As a matter of fact, John the Baptist was so important that he was the one who baptized Jesus. This is so crazy to comprehend but it's true.

If John the Baptist baptized the Savior of the world then he would be considered a man of great faith. That's the guy you call when you are in need of prayer. If anyone has access to the throne room of God it has to be John the Baptist. However, something happened from the time that John baptized Jesus in Matthew chapter three and Matthew chapter eleven because John finds himself in some dire circumstances. Both Jesus and John went on to have dynamic ministries. However, John finds himself in prison for doing what God told him to do. Therefore his faith began to waiver. He began to question the very message that he had been preaching. So he asks himself the question that most Christians are guilty of asking; "Do I really believe this Jesus stuff"?

Timeout! Let's pump the brakes for a moment

We all come to this crossroad in our lives where we have to decide if we really believe this Jesus stuff. You may have been a Christian for a long time – but you will still face this at some point in your life. For some of you, you are facing it right now. So you've got to have a John the Baptist moment. If you've never had a John the Baptist moment, you're not breathing.

"When John heard in prison what Christ was doing, he sent his disciples to ask him, "Are you the one who was to come, or should we expect someone else"?" Matthew 11:2-3

The man that baptized Jesus, the man who literally saw the Holy Spirit land on Jesus, is now questioning Jesus. Now we can't beat up John over this because we are guilty of doing the same thing. We have seen God work in our lives and in other people's lives and we still allow our faith to be shaken. We still question whether this Jesus stuff is real or not.

Let me be clear and blunt: This Christian life is full of ups and downs. John, who was the greatest man born of a woman, found himself in prison for following what God told him to do. So let me ask you;

what's your prison today? Is it family issues, disappointments, discouragement, depression, conflict with a friend, a bad mistake that you made and it's eating your conscience alive? Whatever it is, it has caused your faith to be shaken and has caused you to question Jesus.

But there's hope in all this. And here's the beautiful thing about having a relationship with Jesus: One day we will stand before God and He's going to unfold everything in your life. Then we will see the big picture and say, "Now I understand why that happened".

Romans 8:28 is a great picture of God's love and concern for us. We will revisit this verse again in the next chapter. This is a verse that I resort to quite a bit in my personal life. Sometimes we just need God's reassurance. Reassurance is what John was searching for while he was in prison. So for now let this verse speak to you. *"And we know that in all things God works for the good of those who love him, who have been called according to his purpose"*.

One of these days our Father in Heaven is going to put all of this together for us and it's going to bring our faith back to full circle. Other people may not get it, but you will. You getting it is all that matters.

Time of reflection

* If Jesus was to give us a one sentence summary about your life, what would He say?
* John the Baptist was a real guy with real feelings. You are a real person with real feelings.

So have you had your John the Baptist moment where you questioned God?

* Replay that in your mind and do some reflecting. What was the situation and what was it like going through it?
* God loves you and He will make sure that you feel loved despite your faith being shaken. What can you do when you have those moments of doubt?
* Romans 8:28 is a favorite verse for many struggling people. I encourage you to underline it or circle it in your Bible. Adopt this verse and make it a part of your life.

Prayer for Batteries

Lord I know that I am weak and I need you to strengthen my faith. There are days when I can hold fast and days when I can let go and question Your goodness. No matter what my eyes may see, let them see You and Your work. Things are going to work for the good because I love You and I know that You love me.

Chapter 3

Adversity: Sometimes Life is Too Much

Great moments in life come through adverse situations

We've all heard the phrase, "God has a purpose for everything that happens to you". That is true but sometimes hard to accept. When we face adversity it is not something we accept with great joy. If the truth was revealed, as humans we try everything to avoid adverse situations. That is unless you're a jerk; which in that case, no one probably likes you. Adversity is real and it is really a part of our everyday lives. If you aren't going through an adverse situation right now, just hold on because it's coming.

I don't know who said it or where I read it, but this has stuck with me for a long time and I wanted to share it with you, *"Great moments in life come through adverse situations"*.

Adversity has a positive side and/or positive outcome. Of course this is a statement that we hear all the time. Our first response to that would be, "Oh really? You don't know what I'm going through!" To see the positive side of adversity is not just wishful thinking or denial of reality. To see the positive side of adversity is a statement of faith. This is hard to wrap our minds around when we are struggling.

The positive side of adversity is based on a couple of beliefs that we must hold onto when dealing with life: (1) God really does have a plan for your life that is bigger than you could ever imagine. With that being said we must understand how this correlates in our day to day activities. If you desire for God's plan to be your plan in your life, then God will do whatever it takes to see His plan fulfilled in your life...... However, sometimes that's going to hurt. If your will is to do God's Will, then God will not go against your will; but He will shuffle things to see His Will done in your life (Yes that's a mouth full. Say that several times out loud). Believing this means that God can use any adversity that comes your way for His plan. He will use your adversities to further your purpose on this earth and work His plan through you. (2) God can make any situation good regardless of how bad the situation is you are in. You may think your life has derailed and you have crashed beyond repair; but scripture tells us to hold on. Here again we will revisit Romans 8:28.

"And we know that in all things God works for the good of those who love him, who have been called according to his purpose".

Adversity: Sometimes Life is Too Much

God has a way of arranging things so that good will come from bad no matter what the circumstances may be. God is bigger and more powerful than anything you are going through. That's why God is known as the Redeemer. He takes what enslaves us and frees us. He brings us into oneness with Himself and He protects us. He desires what's best for us.... even if it does hurt.

"Praise the Lord, O my soul, and forget not all his benefits – who forgives all your sins and heals all your diseases, who redeems your life from the pit and crowns you with love and compassion, who satisfies your desires with good things so that your youth is renewed like the eagle's. The LORD works righteousness and justice for all the oppressed". Psalm 103:2-6

I don't have the authority to add to scripture, but I do understand that when God makes a promise, He makes a promise. When God redeems a situation, He sends a message to other people who are observing your life and observing to see if God is really going to work. Through that message from God, there will be many different reactions: from conviction to repentance to praise. Our life is a reflection of the character and nature of the faith we profess. How we handle every situation in life tells a story. What story do you want told about yourself?

When God provides us with a breakthrough, it is not limited to just us. When God pulls us out of an adverse situation, yes, it benefits us in a major way, but it also can have an impact on others. Many times in my life I've been through issues that I thought I could not make it through. When reaching the peak of each situation, and almost every time, someone will ask me how I made it through. My point is this: People are watching you. As a Christian you are under a microscope. The world outside the realm of your own reality is watching to see how you handle each situation and they are curious of whether or not your God is real, much less big enough to get you through. Jesus taught this to His disciples through a blind man in Jerusalem. Even the disciple wanted to see the outcome of this man's adversity

"As he went along, he saw a man blind from birth. His disciples asked him, "Rabbi, who sinned, this man or his parents, that he was born blind"." John 9:1-2

The disciples wanted to know whose sin caused the man to be born blind. Why did the man's blindness have to be the result of someone's sin? Evidently the disciples had been taught all their lives that illness was a sign of God's judgment. I'm not sure where this form of teaching comes from. Yes, sin nature is passed down from generation to generation; but I find it hard to accept that God would cause a child to be born blind to punish the child for something the parents had done. Many times circumstances are just out of our control and out of our understanding. The disciples just knew for certain that someone's sin caused this man to be blind. And in the man's defense....

Adversity: Sometimes Life is Too Much

what did he do so terrible while he was in his mother's womb that caused him to be born blind. He was born blind, so how could he have anything wrong? Do you ever think that Jesus just gave His disciples "that look"? You know the one I'm talking about. That look that your parents used to give you when you asked something stupid. Look at what Jesus told them.

"Neither this man nor his parents sinned, but this happened so that the work of God might be displayed in his life". John 9:3

Ever made mud pies?

There was a purpose to the man's adversity. The disciples saw his blindness as being caused by something bad. Jesus taught that the man's blindness was so that God could do something great....and maybe teach the disciples a lesson on jumping to conclusion. Your adverse situation is a golden opportunity for God to display His power in and through you. We tend to jump to conclusions when bad things happen in our lives or in the lives of those we are in contact with. Why is it that God is always the first one to get thrown under the bus? The sad thing is it's mostly by "Christians". We trust and love God when things are going great in life, but the moment that life appears to go haywire we lose all sense of trust and love.

I want you to notice that Jesus did not say, "This man is blind because he was such a bad person, but God is going to use his bad situation anyway". I want you to notice that Jesus did not say, "Yeah, his parents made some stupid decisions when they were younger so God is punishing them and their son; but I think I will heal him anyway". That would be much easier for us and the disciples to accept. Jesus said that God had a purpose much higher than what we and the disciples could ever imagine. God used this miracle to bring something positive and eternal in the man's life and in the lives of the people who witnessed the healing. Even the religious leaders were flabbergasted by this miracle.

> *"How then were your eyes opened, they demanded. He replied, "The man they call Jesus made some mud and put it on my eyes. He told me to go to Siloam and wash. So I went and washed, and then I could see".*
> John 9:10-11

Jesus made mud pies. How stinking awesome is that? When I was a kid I used to make mud pies.... except I ate them instead of trying to perform a miracle with them. Although, I did use them to throw at my little brother.....and my aim was so bad that it did take a miracle if I hit him with one.

What Jesus said about the man born blind and did for him should put a new light on any type of adversity we experience. Yes, we need to be concerned about our adversity, but we should be more concerned with the results from our adversity. We should not let adversity throws us back, defeat us, or pull us down. As Christians, we should look at adversity as something that will make us stronger (spiritually and emotionally), better (as a Christian) and an all-around better person.

What can I learn from my situation(s)?

No one in their right frame of mind likes adversity in their lives. We don't wake up and say, "Yep! I sure hope today is the worst day ever; It would be so awesome if I walked outside and had a flat tire; I sure hope my boss chews me out really good as soon as I get to work; I love bad news". That would make us into a complete idiot. However, valuable lessons can be learned through adversity if we allow our faith to do its part. Adversity can show us how to fully be the Christian that God wants us to be and how to hold onto the faith that we profess. There's not a magic formula to overcoming adversity, but it does require a lot of faith and patience when you're going through it.

I know you're thinking to yourself right now, "Logan you don't know what I'm going through". You are absolutely right. I don't know. I can promise you this; your current situation doesn't have to be the outcome of your life. Don't let what you're going through define who or what you become. Never accept less than God has for you. God has a plan and a purpose for your life. God can use whatever comes against you for your good. God will use your current situation to not only touch your life, but touch those who are watching how you handle it. So many times the things that happen in our lives affect everyone around us.

I want you to think about this and about how we let our situations control our attitudes: Ask yourself this question and do an honest evaluation, *"What has more control over my life, my situation or my faith in Jesus"*. Maybe you just need for Jesus to make some mud pies in your life. I want you to think about how ridiculous this sounds; Jesus put mud on a guy's face and he was healed. Mud. Yes, we know the mud within itself had no healing power, so don't be going all theological on me, but the man believed what Jesus told him. So the man went and washed in Siloam and was healed. It wasn't the water that healed him either. It was his faith and his belief in what Jesus told him. The man had to take a little initiative in this process. Hint, Hint. You get what I'm saying?

What we let control us will show what we really hold on to. Bad things just happen. Our faith in the Almighty God should be what we focus our time and energy on. We don't have to be negative over our bad luck. God will bring you out of the bad situation you are in when you take some initiative and be obedient to what He tells you to do. Here's the beautiful thing about God working in your life is this; when God brings you out, He brings you *all* the way out.

Be willing to learn

The first step to learning is acknowledging that you need to learn. If we are willing to acknowledge that our adverse situation can bring something positive in our lives and that God desires for us to be more like Christ, then we can ask ourselves; what is the reason for this adversity in my life? No one faced more adversity on this earth than Jesus Himself. The

One who gave up His glory and His throne in Heaven to live as a poor man and face adversity every day. Yet, that's who God desires for us to immolate in our lives. Jesus is the greatest lesson on adversity. Yes, there are tons of stories in the Bible about people who lived their entire lives and ministries in hard to deal with circumstances. With that being said, none of them willingly gave up Heaven. Did you get that? Jesus willingly gave up Heaven to live in adversity because He desired to be the God that truly loves His creation.

There's a major lesson in that. Jesus is a teacher. Not only is Jesus a teacher, but is referred to as the "Good Teacher" by the rich young ruler in Luke 18:18. Because Jesus was and is actually more than the good teacher, He can show us that our adverse situations can and will give us new insight and understanding about ourselves that can change our attitude toward Him. Jesus is the One we must look to when going through adversity. Why? Because He knows a little bit about adversity and rough situations.

This is just a thought as we close out this chapter: Do you ever think that God allows adversity to get our attention? I'm asking you this just from personal experiences. Many times in my life I have lost focus of what God has told me to do. It never fails that during that time of lost focus something will happen that causing me to zoom back in on God....then the pain of the situation will cease. This has happened more times than I would like to admit.

"Show me your ways, O LORD, teach me your paths; guide me in your truth and teach me,

for you are God my Savior, and my hope is in you all day long". Psalm 25:4-5

*It doesn't take a rocket scientist to see the pattern here. Show, teach, and guide....and teach again.

As a teacher of the Bible (especially when teaching students) I can tell you that my first goal is to get the student's attention. Even when teaching adults the first priority is to get their attention. We live in an attention deficit time. People just don't listen. A person who isn't listening or paying attention will not learn. So maybe, just maybe God sometimes uses adversity in our lives to get our attention.

Time of reflection

* What is the adverse situation that you're going through right now; or maybe have just currently came out of?
* Think about your circle of influence (we will talk about influence a little later). Now think about how you handle life when it comes at you unexpectedly. In recent times, has your adversity determined who you are or did your faith determine who you are? Remember; people are watching you.
* Sometimes God's intention is to get our attention. Listen closely to what God has to say and watch closely to what God is trying to show you.

Adversity: Sometimes Life is Too Much

* Don't resist the lesson through your situations. Yes it hurts and it is very painful. But I promise that if you go at it like it depends on God, you will look back and receive a valuable lesson.
* Don't pray that God would keep your life free from adversity, but that you will grow from adversity.

Prayer for Batteries

Lord, adversity is blinding sometimes. When circumstances arise I admit that I tend to get aggravated with live and the faith I claim to profess. Guide me through each situation with Your mercy and grace. It is only by Your strength that I can get through. I know I can't do this on my own. So whenever an adverse situation comes my way help me to use it for Your glory so that others can come to know You through my situations.

Chapter 4

Surrender

Commitment versus surrender

There's a difference between commitment and surrender. When you commit to something you are technically still in control. But when you surrender you are fully giving yourself over. So don't be deceived by your own lie. Surrender causes you to lose control.

So let me ask you: have you committed to Jesus or have you surrendered to Him?

Let's break it down like this: You can commit to getting up early every day and working out. You can commit to reading a book. You can commit to being successful. You can commit to growing closer to God. But always remember; commitment is only as good as the person making the commitment. So what happens the first time you over sleep and miss a workout? What happens when you're too busy to finish that book that you've started? What happens the first time you hit a bump in the road and face major discouragement? What happens when God doesn't work in a way that you think He should? That's why I said that a commitment is only as good as the person making the commitment. Again, commitment and surrender is not the same thing. So don't lie to yourself.

Surrender = to give up, to relinquish, to abandon yourself[3]

In the Old Testament book of First Kings there's a short story about the calling of God on the prophet Elisha (not Elijah, but Elisha). This short story is often overlooked because it is contained in only three verses. However, it has a huge impact on the difference between commitment and surrender. Elijah was the one who basically commissioned him, but this story revolves around Elisha's obedience to surrender. Elisha didn't make a commitment to God's calling, but surrendered everything he had and even known to God's calling. So as we walk through this together, be sure that you get the "sh" and the "j" separated so that we will know who we are talking about.

"So Elijah went up from there and found Elisha son of Shaphat. He was plowing with twelve yoke of oxen, and he himself was driving the twelfth pair. Elijah went up to him and threw his cloak around him. Elisha then left his oxen and ran after Elijah. "Let me kiss my father and mother good-bye," he said,

---

[3] Webster's Dictionary & Thesaurus. Surrender. Polskabook. Poland. 2006. 381.

*"and then I will come with you." "Go back,"
Elijah replied. "What have I done to you?"
So Elisha left him and went back. He took his
yoke of oxen and slaughtered them. He burned
the plowing equipment to cook the meat and
gave it to the people, and they ate. Then he
set out to follow Elijah and became his attendant"*. 1 Kings 19:19-21

In life it's so hard to let go of everything that we know and have. It's even harder when you're doing it to follow after something you've only heard about and not seen. That's why it's called surrender because you're giving up everything to follow Jesus. You can't hold on to what you think is right or wrong. You have to let go and let Jesus have full control of your life.

Here's the thing about Elisha: He was young and evidently wealthy if he had a family farm and farming equipment. But when God spoke to him and said, "I want you", he burned his plows and killed all the bulls and didn't look back.

This is a big deal

I grew up in a farming community in the Delta region of Arkansas so I know why this is such a big deal. If you were in a farming family you had it made. I mean it was hard work but you had it made. This is why; you knew you would always have a job with a great income. The farming life gets passed down from generation to generation to generation. So leaving your family business behind and burning everything is kind of a big deal. Kids that went to college where I grew up, most of them got a degree in agriculture or business, (some even combined the degree to agricultural business) so that they could come back home and run the family farm. Now that you know that, can't you see why this is such a big deal for Elisha to surrender everything to follow God's calling on his life?

The Apostle Paul is probably one of the greatest role models in the Bible, especially the New Testament, when it comes to surrendering it all for the sake of Christ. He gives us encouragement through some powerful words in Philippians 3:7-9. *"But whatever was to my profit I now consider loss for the sake of Christ. What is more, I consider everything a loss compared to the surpassing greatness of knowing Christ Jesus my Lord, for whose sake I have lost all things. I consider them rubbish, that I may gain Christ and be found in him, not having a righteousness of my own that comes from the law, but that which is through faith in Christ – the righteousness that comes from God and is by faith"*.

Too many people commit to things and at the first sign of adversity they bail out of their own commitment. However, when you surrender you're burning everything that your heart is still holding on to. When you burn the plow and kill the bulls you are completely giving yourself over to Jesus and giving yourself over to whatever He's asked you to do. Think about this; if Jesus has asked you to do something, don't you think He's going to make sure you're equipped to do it?

A long time ago I surrendered my "yes and my life" to God. Let me explain that: I told God that whatever He asked me to do the answer would automatically be yes. So in essence, I've said yes before He's even asked. I admit that it's a little intimidating and scary. You've got to surrender your yes to God and burn the plows that you're holding onto. That's what Elisha did and that's what the Apostle Paul did. Elisha did what he had to do and didn't turn back. Paul said that he considers everything a loss just to know Jesus. Paul said he would get rid of everything in his life if it kept him from surrendering his life to Jesus. What are you willing to surrender to God; your talents, your money, your calling, what is it that you have in your life that God wants to use?

Let me tell you why Elisha burned all of his farm equipment and killed his tractors. Because he knew that his heart and his mind would be focused on those things instead of God. And that's where some of you are at right now. You're focused on the plow and you won't let it go. You may even be working for the Kingdom of God and serving and doing some great things for Jesus, but your focus is still on the plow because you didn't burn it. So if you truly want to be effective you've got to burn everything that hinders your life from truly living for Jesus. It may be quitting a job, ending a relationship, or cutting ties in another area of your life. There's an old saying, "don't burn your bridges". Well, sometimes you have to burn your bridges to keep form going back across them because some of those bridges lead you back to a life that is not surrendered to Jesus.

You are either in this thing with Jesus or you aren't. You can't continue to hold on to the things

Surrender

that are keeping you from Jesus. You need to burn your plows and kill your bulls – don't even look back – surrender your life to Jesus and follow Him. You've got to quit jacking around. A life with Jesus is not a game. You can't push pause or call a timeout. You either surrender to Him or you don't. It's not about commitment, it's about surrender. Too many people commit to Jesus, but not enough surrender to Jesus.

Nothing is more important in your life than a relationship with Jesus. I'm not talking about going to church or acting a certain way. Anyone can do that. I'm talking about fully surrendering your life to the One who died on a cross for you. You got to burn the plows and throw off everything that is hindering you from truly knowing Jesus. Elisha went back home and threw off everything that he knew would hinder him from serving the King of Kings and the Lord of Lords. In the book of Hebrews chapter twelve the writer says to throw off everything that hinders us. Then the writer tells us to fix our eyes on Jesus.

What's stopping you from knowing Jesus? Not knowing about Him; but surrendering your life to Him? What is hindering you? What is the plow in your life that you're holding onto that you just can't seem to let go of? Don't commit to Jesus, surrender to Jesus. Look again at what Elisha did to ensure that nothing got in the way of his heart for God.

> *"So Elisha left him and went back. He took his yoke of oxen and slaughtered them. He burned the plowing equipment to cook the meat and gave it to the people, and they ate. Then he set*

out to follow Elijah and became his attendant".
1 Kings 19:21

Time of reflection

* Take a few moments and reflect on your life and your current circumstances. What are the plows in your life that you're holding onto?
* Why is it that you look for security in your plows and not in what God has called you to do?
* This is a hard concept to grasp. Letting go of everything to follow Jesus is crazy. But it's worth the ride.
* What can you do differently to move from commitment to surrender?
* What bridges do you keep going back across that also need to be burned with the plows.

Prayer for Batteries

Lord, forgive me for merely committing to You and not surrendering to You. Help me to grasp the difference in my everyday life. Each day when I wake up help me to surrender the day to You. Give me the boldness to burn the plows in my life that need to be burned. This is going to be a hard process, but I trust Your guidance and Your will. Father, take my life and use it to Your glory. Help me to not look back.

Chapter 5

Worship

I read this story a long time ago and I can't remember where I got it from, but as I thought about worship and sitting through church this story kept replaying in my mind. A little boy asked his mother what was the highest number she'd ever counted to. She said she really didn't know so she asked him the same question. Then he said, "5,372". His mother asked him why he didn't make it any farther. He then said, "because church was over". Evidently he was bored.

True worship

True worship is not boring. When you truly worship, God will not allow you to get bored. But…..worship begins with your attitude. The Psalmist described a type of worship that is true and authentic, and absolutely not boring.

"Come, let us sing for joy to the LORD; let us shout aloud to the ROCK of our salvation. Let us come before him with thanksgiving and extol him with music and song. For the LORD is the great God, the great king above all gods. In his hands are the depths of the earth, and the mountain peaks belong to him. The sea is his, for he made it, and his hands formed the dry land. Come, let us bow down and worship, let us kneel before the LORD our Maker;" Psalm 95:1-6

Do you understand the concept of worship and the concept of church and why we assemble together? The word "worship" is used over 250 times in the Bible. So it's kind of a big deal. So how would you define the word "worship"? Would you say that it's just singing? Or maybe just giving? What about surrendering (which we just finished a chapter on)? Or is worship just standing in "awe" of all that God has done?

How or why should we worship? Let's break down the previous verses. See what you can pull out of them that tells us how or why we should worship: we worship through music, we worship with thanksgiving, we worship by praising, we worship God because He is the Creator, and we worship because He is our Maker. What else needs to be said? The Psalmist understood the concept of worship and that we should desire to worship the Great Author of our lives.

The Abraham Factor

Something interesting to note is that the first time the word worship is used is in Genesis twenty-two when God told Abraham to sacrifice his son on a mountain.

"Early the next morning Abraham got up and saddled his donkey. He took with him two of his servants and his son Isaac. When he had cut enough wood for the burnt offering, he set out for the place God had told him about. On the third day Abraham looked up and saw the place in the distance. He said to his servants, "Stay here with the donkey while I and the boy go over there. We will worship and then we will come back to you"." Genesis 22:3-5

There's a couple of things I want you to pull out of these three verses on worship.

Before we get back to the scripture, let me illustrate it like this: Have you ever gone shopping and the salesperson said, "Can I help you find something specific"? And then you say something ridiculous like, "No. I'll know it when I see it". That's kind of like worship. You'll know it when you experience it. Sometimes we struggle with worship. We struggle with getting into the mood and the mode of worship. Then something clicks inside of our hearts and minds and we begin to pour our hearts out to God – we begin to worship. It doesn't have to be at church when this happens. Worship can happen anywhere. You can

Batteries Not Included

worship in your car driving down the road. One of the greatest experiences in worship I've ever had was travelling to my daughter's basketball game and I was listening to a Hillsong CD and the Spirit just overtook me. I was whipping tears and praying and praising all at the same time. God was with me and I experienced true worship. I worshipped in Spirit and Truth as Jesus told the woman at the well (John 4). You can also worship while doing laundry or cleaning around the house. You can even worship while going through adverse circumstances. Worship begins with your attitude.

Abraham did not know where he was going and I want you to get this. The story says that Abraham looked up and saw the place. He had that, "that's it" moment that I talked about earlier. He knew at that moment that he saw where God was leading him to worship. When he saw where he was to go worship he knew it. He had the "that's it" moment.

Now I want you to notice that he wasn't going to return until he worshipped. *"We will worship and then we will come back to you"*. He said, "we will go worship". Abraham's main goal was to worship. That's it. Worship. Here's something key to Abraham that we must experience if we are ever going to truly worship: Think about the most important thing or person in your life. Worship starts with sacrifice and surrender.

Please get this: singing songs doesn't necessarily mean you are worshipping. You can know every word to every Christian song and every word to every hymn and still not be worshipping God. You're going to have to place your prized possession before God and surrender it. Then you can worship. Until then you

Worship

are just going through the motions. Worship is giving more than yourself over to God. Worship is eliminating all distractions. Remember, worship starts with our attitude.

Is it possible that you've never really had a worship experience? Could it be because you're trying to fill that void with things that have nothing to do with God? What scares me the most about church people is that they honestly believe that because they show up, pay tithes, and know how to get around in their Bibles that they are worshipping. Worshipping is encountering God and knowing that you've had an experience that is basically unexplainable. If you leave a church service and you can't say that you met with a Holy God....I hate to be the bearer of bad news, but you probably didn't experience true worship.

Let's close out this chapter with this thought: God does not want you having things in your heart and in your life that you worship more than Him. The word "worship" comes from two words: *"worth"* and *"ship"*. So if something or someone is "worth" more to you than God you will never experience worship.

Some of us never experience true worship because you are just spectating. Maybe it's because we just stand there twiddling our fingers. You've got to stop spectating and start participating. Worship is not a spectator sport, it's a participator sport. So get in the game and get your attitude focused on worshipping the One who made you and longs for your worship.

Time of Reflection

* In your own opinion; what is your definition of "worship"
* Has it ever clicked? Have you had that moment when you truly worshipped? If you have, reflect on it for a few moments.
* Why do you think Abraham was so confident that he and the boy would worship and return? You may need to reread the story.
* What is your "worth" "ship" that you are holding onto? Is it God or something else?
* We can't worship what we don't know. So here's my question to you: do you know God? Not know about God; but KNOW God?

Prayer for Batteries

Lord, I want to experience worship that is true and genuine. Help me to have an Abraham type of experience where I know that I am about to worship You. Let me come under the understanding that worship starts in my heart and that it's not about me but about You. Lord, let You be my "worth" "ship" and nothing else.

Chapter 6
Influence

Everyone has influence. You may not think that you do, but you do. Here's the catch: your influence is either positive or negative. There's no in between. So how would you describe the type of influence you have?

Whether you know it or not, you're an influencer

Do you know the difference between a thermostat and a thermometer? A thermometer merely tells what the temperature is in a particular area. If your thermometer reads seventy-five degrees and you place it in a room with a different temperature, the thermometer will change to whatever the room temperature is. It always adjusts to its environment. The thermostat, however, adjusts the room temperature. If the thermostat is set at seventy-five degrees and the room is eighty degrees, the temperature of the room changes to match to whatever the thermostat says. The room will become seventy-five degrees. The thermometer is influenced by the environment; whereas, the thermostat controls the environment.

You live your life as either a thermostat or a thermometer. You can either blend in with the crowd, or you can change the crowd. You are either influencing others, or they are influencing you. That's a pretty powerful concept to wrap your mind around. We all have influence, but it's what we control or what we let control that determines where we stand temperature wise.

Salt and light; or no salt and no light

In my opinion, one of Jesus' greatest teachings on influence lies in the passage where He taught about salt and light. Right after giving the Beatitudes Jesus moves right into influence. Jesus knew that the disciples and those under His voice would have some sort of significant influence in their circle of acquaintances. Just like us as individuals today, we have influence on a circle of people, and then one person of our circle has influence on a circle of people.....and so and so on. You get the picture. We have influence that leads to multiple people being under our influence.

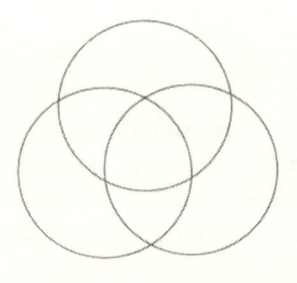

Influence

Influence is a powerful thing. We control the environment; or, the environment will control us. Be the influencer not the influencey.

"You are the salt of the earth. But if the salt loses its saltiness, how can it be made salty again? It is no longer good for anything, except be thrown out and trampled by men. You are the light of the world. A city on a hill cannot be hidden. Neither do people light a lamp and put it under a bowl. Instead they put it on its stand, and it gives light to everyone in the house. In the same way, let your light shine before men, that they may see your good deeds and praise your father in heaven."
Matthew 5:13-16

Influence = "the power to affect others"[4]

What is the key to influence? I asked you that because we all know whether or not we're surrounded by the right people. We know whether or not we're surrounded by the wrong people. One thing is always going to happen: You will either influence them or they will influence you. People of good influence will take you to the next level, whereas people of bad influence will bring you down.

Great influencers don't make excuses, they make things better. Great influencers don't tear people down; they lead them to where they need to be. There

---

[4] Webster's Dictionary & Thesaurus. Influence. Polskabook. Poland. 2006. 193.

Batteries Not Included

are people in this world who need to be influenced by those who believe in God and are in love with Jesus. So do you understand the power of influence?

One of the keys to influence is how you handle certain situations and how you react when the pressures of life are on you. People are watching you because you're an influencer. So as people observe you they will come to the conclusion about who you really are....whether positive or negative; and that's influence. So it's up to you to give people the proper conclusion about who you are. There have been so many reputations damaged because of one bad decision or because someone said the wrong thing in the heat of the moment. With that thought there's also been a lot of reputations saved because the person made the right decision and thought it through logically. So always take a deep breath and consider the influence that you possess.

The power of influence is too strong to ignore. If someone ever tells you that young people are the only ones who struggle with this, they are lying. Everyone is influenced by another person in some way. It doesn't matter how independent a person appears to be. We are all looking for that influence. Your age and your hierarchy in your job or position is thrown out the window when it comes to influence. Always remember, your title or position does not give you the type of influence that God wants you to possess. Yes, your self-imposed pedestal can give you influence; but is it the "light of the world" influence?

God knows that influence can work for good or for bad. Would you consider yourself salt and light? This is a fine line because Jesus said if the salt loses

Influence

its saltiness it is no longer good for anything. Those are strong words. I never want my savior to say of me, "You are no longer good for anything". You should strive for Jesus to never have to say that of you.

Time of reflection

* Where does our influence lie? Are you a good influencer or a bad influencer?
* How can you be a better influencer to those you come in contact with every day?
* What can you do differently tomorrow than what you did today that will impact someone's life?
* What areas of your life are people really watching?
* Are you a thermometer (influenced by others) or a thermostat (you control the environment)?

Prayer for Batteries

Lord, let me not ever be the one who is influenced in a negative way. I desire to be used by You and be the one who influences my circle to walk with You. As situations come my way guard my actions so that I may react in a way that pleases You. You are the ultimate influencer! As I grow to be more like Your Son, let me have the type of influence that will make an impact for eternal purposes only. I know that others are watching me; so as they watch me let them see You in me.

Chapter 7

Forgiveness

℘

Forgiveness starts with myself

Forgiveness starts in the heart of a person and moves to the mind. Forgiveness is a big deal. It starts with the inner being of a person. The forgiveness that we are going to talk about is personal forgiveness. The things that we have going on in our own lives. Maybe you're reading this right now and are being eaten alive by something. You are living in guilt right now over some things you have done or may be currently involved in. The emotions of your life rise and falls more than the stock market.

What do we do when we mess up? Where do we go when we have failed God? What about when we have failed ourselves? Do we hide in a closet until the pain goes away? Or, do we face the situation knowing that forgiveness is actually seeking us?

So what happens when we try to push through without asking for forgiveness and receiving forgiveness? Here's something pretty deep to think about; you can ask for it and not receive it. Here's why, it's not that God won't forgive you, because He will forgive you immediately if you ask for forgiveness in a genuine way. The problem in us not receiving forgiveness is that we can't forgive ourselves. Until you can forgive yourself, you will never experience true forgiveness. When God forgives you, you have to also forgive yourself, or whatever it is that you are dealing with will continue to eat you alive from the inside out.

A guilty conscience is pure agony. Until you release that to God you will never be able to live with yourself and you will be a miserable person. The next thing you know you will be sitting on your front porch rocking in your chair mad at the world and will be a bitter old man or old woman. However, living a life of peace knowing that you have been forgiven is a beautiful thing. God does not want us to be bitter... God wants us to be forgiven and enjoy the embrace of His fellowship. King David said some of the most heart-felt words that we find in the scriptures.

"Blessed is he whose transgressions are forgiven, whose sins are covered. Blessed is the man whose sin the LORD does not count against him and in whose spirit is no deceit. When I kept silent my bones wasted away through my groaning all day long. For day and night your hand was heavy upon me; my strength was sapped as in the heat of summer. Then I acknowledged my sin to you and did

not cover up my iniquity. I said, "I will confess my transgressions to the LORD" – and you forgave the guilt of my sin." Psalm 32:1-5

I want you to notice how David started this off the first two verses. He said, "Blessed". The word blessed in this context means "happy". Happy is the person whose sins are forgiven. That's what he's saying. I'm now happy within myself because I've been forgiven. The reason he was so happy is because up to this point David was miserable and living in pure agony. How do we know David was miserable? Because many Bible scholars believe that Psalm thirty-two is the sequel to Psalm fifty-one; in which both are in conjunction with David's terrible acts in his pursuit of another man's wife. Yes I know that the numerical part of this is backwards, but that's just how it is. In Psalm fifty-one David finally confessed his sins to God about all the ungodly things that he had done in conjunction with Bathsheba.

Personal confession hurts

The agony of a guilty conscience is rough. The agony that eats our mind can sometimes be worse than any physical ailments. Think about what David said in Psalm 32 when he said that his bones wasted away because he was silent about his sins and that the hand of God was so heavy on him that he couldn't function properly. Because he was silent and because he tried to deal with this on his own and not confess his sins to God and seek forgiveness, his mind caused his bones to waist away. His mind caused him to have not only psychological problems, but physical problems.

Let me illustrate this is a way that may make this a little clearer to you: There are things in life that will cause your mind to affect the rest of your body. One is guilt over sin that you have committed. To put this on a simpler level; when someone close to you dies or you've had your heart broken by someone, it affects your mind so much that it trickles down to your appetite and then to your physical health. You can't eat and you can't sleep. When those things begin to happen your physical health turns bad. The body doesn't function like it's supposed to. I know this first hand. I've experienced heartbreak and faced major disappointments in my life that have affected my mind so bad that it ruined my appetite to the point where I couldn't eat or drink anything for days. All I wanted to do was lie in bed and groan about my circumstances. I didn't want to see anyone or talk to anyone. I didn't even want to talk to God. This not only affects your mind but also your body. If you've been there then you know exactly what I'm talking about. That's exactly why David said his bones wasted away. He was struggling with some severe depression. It was so bad that he couldn't even function.

What you are about to see is what took place right in the middle of David's struggle. He tried covering up his wrongs but God was all over this dude. It was because David tried covering it all up, his conscience was eating him alive. So let's take a glimpse into this story out of Second Samuel chapter twelve.

"David pleaded with God for the child. He fasted and went into his house and spent the nights lying on the ground. The elders of his household stood beside him to get him up from the ground, but he refused, and he would not eat any food with them. On the seventh day the child died. David's servants were afraid to tell him the child was dead, for they thought, "While the child was still living, we spoke to David but he would not listen to us. How can we tell him the child is dead? He may do something desperate"."

Here is arguably the greatest king the world has ever seen. Here is the guy that God said was a man after His very heart. Here is a man that as a boy killed a giant that an entire army was scared of. Here is a man that would be a grandfather to Jesus....yes Jesus! So now he is so distraught and in utter depression that he is lying face down on the ground in his own filth. He hasn't eaten, he hasn't taken a bath, and he won't even acknowledge the people who are trying to help him. As a matter of fact, his servants are afraid to tell him the child is dead because they think that the king will commit suicide.

This is serious

So why did this affect David so bad? According to Psalm thirty-two verse four, David said that God's hand was so heavy upon him that it completely zapped all his energy. David even compared it to

Forgiveness

the summer heat beating down on him. I've never been dehydrated or had a heat stroke, but I personally know people who have. I've been told that it feels like you are dying. They've told me that your body doesn't function properly because the body has to pull resources from unusual places. So if David's sin and his conscious was eating at him to the point where he became dehydrated, then I can completely understand why he was confined to the floor.

There have been times in my life and circumstances that I have brought upon myself that I have thought I wouldn't make it through. I have laid in the bed before begging God for healing and for Him to remove the situation. I was not at the level David was at because I never had another man killed because I wanted his wife. I've never had a child die. However, in my mind and I'm sure also in yours, there have been times that our brain and our heart has told you that it was just as bad. You're begging and pleading with a merciful God but it seems that you get no relief. I was listening to T. D. Jakes preach on the passage out of Second Samuel and he posed this question to his congregation and it has been stuck in my mind ever since; He said in essence, "What do you do when you're praying for something to have life that God has already ordained to be dead?".

That is some powerful stuff and I can't rack my brain enough to come up with an answer. I've studied that passage repeatedly because I wanted to answer it. Now I'm not bold enough to give the great Bishop Jakes a call and tell him I need an answer, but I sure do want to understand it for myself. A little side note, I love to hear that dude preach. He inspires me.

Back to David and him laying around in his filthy clothes and his nappy hair: It wasn't until David realized what was going on in his heart and in his mind that he was able to ask for forgiveness. God was all over this dude. Is God all over you right now about something? It was then that David asked for forgiveness and then he was able to say "blessed". When you're forgiven and you know that you've been forgiven, then you can say "blessed". Then you can say, "Now I am happy". Then you can say the very words of David from Psalm fifty-one verse twelve, *"Restore to me the joy of your salvation"*. Those key words I want you to get...."joy and salvation". Forgiveness gives us "joy in our salvation".

It may take God breaking you down, but once you turn it over to God, He's the only one that can give you real joy in life. You learn from your agony. You learn from your anguish. You learn from your mistakes. And then you move on. That's the time you move on in the direction that God would have you go. Forgiveness starts with you. Forgiveness starts in your heart and in your mind. Yes it is a big deal.

Time of reflection

* Honestly evaluate yourself for a few moments. What is it that is eating at you right now?
* Now ask yourself this; "Why do I continue to struggle with this when God will forgive me"?

* Are you "happy" or "blessed" in your life right now? Why or why not?
* Think about the question that Bishop Jakes posed at his congregation. To refresh your memory, *"What do you do when you're praying for something to have life that God has already ordained to be dead?"* Relate that to something within your own personal life. How does this affect how you plead with God over a situation?
* What is it going to take in your life for you to enjoy the joy of your salvation?
* Forgiveness starts with you. You have to forgive yourself. But you also have to forgive others as well. Who is it that you need to forgive and what is it that you need to let go of?

Prayer for Batteries

Lord, help me to accept the fact that I can't change the past; but in the same breath, help me to move on from my mistakes and hold to Your promises. I know You have forgiven me and restored me. Thank You for the mercy You displayed by sending Your Son to the cross to pay for my sins. Clear my conscience and renew my spirit. I now lay this agony at Your alter. Restore to me the joy of my salvation.

Chapter 8

Loving Others

Loving others is something that should just come automatic as a Christian; but it's harder than it appears. Sometimes it's just hard to love other people, especially those that are unlovable. We know that we should do it but we still struggle with it. I have to admit that I'm so guilty of saying, "I love everyone", but more often than not do I genuinely show it. It's even been said that you can love everyone, but that doesn't mean that you have to like them. I guess there's truth in that.

How do we love others

We are going to walk through a couple of basic principles and use a couple of brief scriptures out of the book of Ruth. After Naomi's husband and two sons died she was in a dilemma. Naomi felt led to basically go back home to her own people and release her daughters-in-law to go back home themselves.

Loving Others

Her two daughters-in-law names were Ruth and Orpah. No not Oprah, but Orpah. The one we are going to focus on is Ruth (whom also the book in the Bible is named after). She shows genuine love by the principles that we will discuss.

The first way that Ruth exemplified love was by sticking with her mother-in-law through these tough times. She didn't have to and she wasn't obligated to, but because she genuinely loved Naomi she stuck with her. Naomi even urged Ruth to go back home to her own people so that she could eventually remarry and start a family of her own. Ruth was not going to have it because she loved Naomi.

"But Ruth replied, "Don't urge me to leave you or turn back from you. Where you go I will go, and where you stay I will stay. Your people will be my people and your God my God. Where you die I will die, and there I will be buried. May the LORD deal with me be it ever so severely, if anything but death separates you and me". When Naomi realized that Ruth was determined to go with her, she stopped urging her." Ruth 1:16-18

Many times life is just hard and we need someone there to stay by us and encourage us. We need them to push us through. So reverse that....we need to be that same person to others as well. Please understand that Ruth did not have to stick with Naomi. Ruth could have gone back to her own people. It was because she loved her mother-in-law so much, she was willing to

Batteries Not Included

stick with her through thick and thin. When you genuinely love others; there's sticking power there. Love for others is an amazing thing. I'm not talking about infatuation; but love that runs deep in our lives and it affects us so much that we care about people and their needs.

Proverbs eighteen verse twenty-four in the Message Bible has this passage translated beautifully. It says, *"Friends come and go, but a true friend sticks by you like family"*. Did you get that? A true friend sticks by you like family. Yes I know that some of us have family that we don't want to stick around; but there is that one person in our family that is the glue to the family. They keep everything going and they hold it all together. Maybe it's one of your grandparents. You know what I'm saying. I can remember so well as a little boy every Sunday after church we would all congregate to my great-grandmother's house for lunch. After lunch all of us kids would play in the yard while the adults took naps. Some of you are laughing right now because this describes your family to a "T". When my great-grandmother passed away the Sunday duty was then given to my grandmother (which was her daughter). Then when her health began to fail her my father took on the role. He is still holding on and maintaining the family atmosphere. I tease my father all the time by telling him, "When you pass away everyone will be on their own because I'm not going to do it". For a side note to that; someone once told me that there's a little truth in every joke.

Are you willing to adjust?

Every day of our lives we have to make adjustments. Some adjustments are small and aren't really a big deal. But others are pretty drastic. Think of it like this; you're running behind one morning and you go out to your car only to notice you have a flat tire. Here's a personal disclaimer to my attitude: There's nothing that tests my Christianity more than a flat tire (golf comes in a close second). With a flat tire now you have to make some huge adjustments to your day. You're already running a little late, so now it's a lot late. The rest of your day will have to be adjusted to the time it's going to take to get your tire changed or fixed.

In everyday life there are a lot of times we adjust an area of our lives in order to meet the needs of other people. Ruth was willing to adjust her upcoming future in order to see that her mother-in-law was not alone. The scripture says that Ruth told Naomi, *"Where you go I will go and where you stay I will stay"*. Ruth was so adamant and bold about this that she went on to say that, *"Your people will be my people"*. So let me throw this question at you: are you willing to love others to the point that it throws you into a complete culture shock? Are you willing to love others to the point that you have to adjust your entire life?

Love is an attitude

What adjustments do you need to make to really love others? Is it your attitude? For many of us, we can't love because we don't have the right attitude to love. Is it how you view other people? For some of us we view people as if they are beneath us and they don't deserve to be loved. Maybe it's how you view God? In our mind is God really a loving God that loves us unconditionally. If we have the proper view of God then we would have the proper perspective on how to love like God loves.

Let me ask you this very tough and self-examining question: If you were God, would you love you? I ask that because if we were to do an honest evaluation of our life, what would we find out about our self that is completely unlovable? Yet, God still loves us. All the nasty, dirty parts of our life that we keep hidden deep, the parts that only we know about, and this God that we serve still loves us. There's are parts of our lives that our husband or wife will never know, our parents will never find out, even the FBI couldn't crack through this part of our life...and God still loves us.

Sometimes love takes us out of our comfort zone. We don't like this; but again it goes back to our attitude. If we are willing to adjust our attitude to God's type of love then we would be willing to break through our comfort zone to ensure others knew that we loved them. Genuine love for others pushes us out of the comfortable areas of our lives. It's easy to remain in the bubble that we've created. It's easy to love those who are close to us. It's easy to love those we are supposed to love. What about the people that don't look like us, or act like us, or talk like us, or even smell like us?

News flash, getting out of our comfort zone; guess what? It's not comfortable. It's not designed to be comfortable. However, it's what we are called to do. Jesus didn't hang around the "church" people. As a matter of fact, Jesus didn't even like the church people. Jesus went to the people that the church people refused to go to because He genuinely loved them.

Be an encouragement

One of the most impactful things that you can do is be encouraging. People all around you are hurting and are beaten down by life. Just one encouraging word can change the trajectory of someone's life. There may be a lot of things that you can't do – but we can all be encouraging and say something nice to someone.

> *"The right word at the right time is like a custom-made piece of jewelry"*. Proverbs 25:11 (The Message Bible)

We can take this a step farther: How about just a smile at someone. It's amazing what a smile can do. I like messing with random people. I know that sounds weird, but I am kind of weird. What I really like doing is when I'm standing in a checkout line and there's a kid sitting in the buggy in front of me.... you know the one I'm talking about....the one who stares a hole in you like they know all your sins. Yep. That's the one. So what I do is make faces at them and get them to smiling and laughing. Then when the parent looks at me I just turn away like I'm in lala land. Therefore, this makes the parent and the child look ridiculous. The kid is laughing and the parent doesn't know why. It's great. You should try it some time. But hey, I made someone smile that day, even if it was a kid.

Even when people mess up and do things that are wrong, we are to continue to love them and encourage them. Why? Because the scriptures tell us that love covers a multitude of wrongs. Plus, if you say that you haven't done anything wrong or that you are the most loveable person in the world, you need to repent because you have a problem with lying.

> *"Above all, love each other deeply, because love covers over a multitude of sins. Offer hospitality to one another without grumbling. Each of you should use whatever gift you have received to serve others, as faithful stewards of God's grace in its various forms. If anyone speaks, they should do so as one who speaks the very words of God. If anyone serves, they should do so with the strength God provides, so that in all things God may be praised through Jesus Christ. To him be the glory and the power for ever and ever. Amen."* 1 Peter 4:8-11

When you are able to love and put others before yourself it is then that you experience joy in life. You want to know what the word "JOY" means? Jesus – Others–Yourself. Pretty simple concept, huh? Our only problem is grasping that. If we can learn to

Loving Others

put Jesus first and others second, then love would come naturally and would experience true joy in our Christian lives. So if you want to have real joy in your life; put Jesus and other people ahead of you.

"then make my joy complete by being like-minded, having the same love, being one in spirit and purpose. Do nothing out of selfish ambition or vain conceit. Rather, in humility consider others better than yourselves. Each of you should look not only to your own interests, but also to the interests of the others."
Philippians 2:2-4

I have an uncle who is the most laid back person I've ever been around. I've never seen him mad or worked up about anything. If you ran in and told him the house was on fire and that he needed to escape immediately…he still wouldn't get in a hurry. I asked him one time, I said, "I've never seen you mad at anyone. I've never seen you show emotions or show any anger whatsoever. How do you do it"? Then he gave me the simplest and most profound answer. As a matter of fact, I was taken back and shocked by it. He said in his laid back voice, "I look at everyone as if they are better than me. I love everyone". Wow. Just wow. So I thought and pondered on his statement. Repeatedly I asked myself, "What would this world be like is most Christians looked at life that way; or even just half of those who claim to be Christians"? We control our environments by how we view others and love them.

Loving others is the key to our Christianity. Always remember this; you can't give away what you don't have. If you don't have the love of Christ in you then you can't genuinely love people like you should. This love thing is a two-way street. Love comes and goes from both directions. The great "love" chapter in First Corinthians chapter thirteen verifies this.

"Love is patient, love is kind. It does not envy, it does not boast, it is not proud. It is not rude, it is not self-seeking, it is not easily angered, it keeps no record of wrongs. Love does not delight in evil but rejoices with the truth. It always protects, always trusts, always hopes, always perseveres."

Those scriptures are a beautiful depiction of what love is and is not. They are in essence the "do's and don'ts" of love. If only we could hinge our Christianity on those concepts that the Apostle Paul taught the church? Just think about it; how much better of a Christian would you be if you genuinely loved others? Not because you read this book or another book on love, but because you loved Jesus so much that you saw others the same way He sees them.

Martin Luther King Jr. said, "Darkness cannot drive out darkness: only light can do that. Hate cannot drive out hate: only love can do that".

Loving Others

Time of Reflection

* Why is it so hard to love people?
* Excluding family and close friends: have you ever had to make an adjustment in your life to meet the needs of someone else?
* Our attitude is probably the biggest hindrance we have when it comes to loving people. What "attitude adjustments" do you need to make to love others?
* If you were Ruth....what would you have done in her situation? Be honest!
* Considering others better than yourself is a hard thing. What areas of your life do you need to work on in order to achieve that?
* Pray through the "do's and don'ts" of love in 1 Corinthians 13:4-7. Ask God to reveal and remove those struggles from your life.

Prayer for Batteries

Lord, help me to first off look at myself. Let my life reflect a life that is full of love. Help me to love others as You love me. Father, even when it's hard to love, instill in me the power for love to flow from me. Guide me into fully understanding the concept of true J.O.Y. Thank You for loving me.

Chapter 9

Jesus Extra

❧

The Jesus Extra concept comes from the work of the Holy Spirit. I really don't know why, but when discussing the Holy Spirit around a conservative group of people they kind of get freaked out. Many Christians treat the Holy Spirit as if He is some sort of infection that you don't want anyone knowing that you have. The Holy Spirit is not a virus. What many have failed to understand (or just blatantly ignore) is that the Holy Spirit is actually God. Yes God! He is the third person in the Holy Trinity. So we need to quit freaking out and losing our minds when someone talks about the Holy Spirit.

The Holy Spirit exists for me

The concept and work of the Holy Spirit is a mysterious thing. It's hard to explain and it's hard to comprehend. It doesn't matter how well you know the Bible or if you have a degree in Theology, describing

Jesus Extra

the Holy Spirit is beyond the human mind. Many analogies and visual illustrations have been used as an attempt to describe the person and the work of the Holy Spirit; but in the end we are still puzzled. However, He exists and is fully alive and He exists for everyone who confesses Christ as Lord of their life. The Holy Spirit is a promise from the lips of Jesus.

John chapter fourteen is a discussion between Jesus and His disciples. In this chapter Jesus just flat out tells them that He is not thinking about leaving them, but that He has to leave them. The disciples didn't understand why Jesus had to leave them. It wasn't until the Holy Spirit fell on them in Acts chapter two that they "got it". And when they were filled with the Holy Spirit, they were filled with so much of Jesus that three thousand people got saved at once.

Think about the power that we possess as believers, but that we never utilize. How much more powerful could you live if you allowed Jesus to pour His Holy Spirit all over you? You see – we want just enough Jesus to get us by. For some reason when Jesus tries to use us we ignore it. When Jesus tells us to truly worship, we ignore it. When Jesus tells us to talk to someone about Him, we ignore it. We ignore Jesus' calling on our lives so hard that we block the Holy Spirit from penetrating us.

You need to understand something: There's a difference between having the Holy Spirit in you and being filled with the Holy Spirit.

So what's the difference?

The moment when you confess Jesus as Lord of your life His Spirit comes to live in you. You have the very Spirit of God dwelling in you. The filling of the Spirit is different. The filling of the Spirit is when God consumes your life so much that the Spirit overflows and everyone around you knows you have something special.

I was discussing this very issue with my pastor Dr. Clayton Sheets. This is what he said about the filling of the Holy Spirit, "Logan, think of it like a cluttered closet. Your life is that closet. When you repent and confess you make room for the Holy Spirit. But, for many of us it's still cluttered in there. The Spirit can't move around and fill you because you haven't removed the clutter from your closet. As you begin to take things out and reorganize – the Spirit begins to fill those empty spaces and eventually you will be filled with the Spirit. Now, you can re-clutter your closet again; not allowing yourself to be filled with the Spirit". The filling of the Spirit is like a seasonal thing where you have your highs and lows and ups and downs. It is possible though to live a life filled with the Holy Spirit and God's presence flowing form your life. It is also possible to live your entire Christian life and never experience the filling of the Spirit. Having the Spirit fill you is not about receiving a Sunday school attendance award or being dunked in water. It's about having something super natural happen in your life.

Let me show you that there is a difference between receiving and having the Holy Spirit and being filled with the Holy Spirit. In John chapter twenty after the resurrection of Jesus, it says that Jesus breathed on His disciples and they received the Holy Spirit.

"Jesus came and stood among them and said, "Peace be with you!" The disciples were overjoyed when they saw the Lord. And again Jesus said, Peace be with you! As the Father has sent me, I am sending you." And with that he breathed on them and said, "Receive the Holy Spirit"." John 20:19b-22

Did you see that? They "received" the Holy Spirit. Reread that and put emphasis on the word "received". What happens next is so cool. Keep in mind that this will be the same group of people, with the exception of a few. They've already received the Holy Spirit, but there's more to come.

"When the day of Pentecost came, they were all together in one place. Suddenly a sound like the blowing of a violent wind came from heaven and filled the whole house where they were sitting. They saw what seemed to be tongues of fire that separated and came to rest on each of them. All of them were filled with the Holy Spirit" Acts 2:1-4a

Now did you see that? They were "filled" with the Holy Spirit. Same group of people, with the exception of a few, went from having the Holy Spirit to being filled with the Holy Spirit. When you are filled with the Holy Spirit it is then that God does some great things in and through you. So how do we attain this?

It's like sitting in a classroom. You have the teacher there present; but you aren't paying attention. Therefore, you aren't being filled with the knowledge that is being taught. You hear it but pay it no attention. Let's even say the pastor is up preaching. We hear him because he is talking, but we are not listening to the spiritual truths that he is sharing. Therefore, we aren't taking anything in. That's how many of us treat the Holy Spirit. We hear what we want and maybe even take in what we want but the Holy Spirit isn't consuming us because we have some sort of block up. The Holy Spirit wants to consume our lives so much that there's an overflow.

As Christians we should be so filled with the Spirit that Jesus jumps out of us onto others. Our lives should be so consumed by the Spirit of God that when people look at us they should be able to see Jesus. It's a crazy concept but a true concept. Even some of the disciples said once that they couldn't help but talk about Jesus. The reason was because there was such an overflow of the Spirit that the overflow had to go somewhere.

"Do not get drunk on wine, which leads to debauchery. Instead, be filled with the Spirit.
Ephesians 5:18

When you're filled with the Spirit you do great things for God and you impact other people's lives. However, when you're filled with other things, those things push the Spirit of God to the side. Your life is cluttered. So why did Paul use the comparison of wine with the Spirit? Because too much wine controls you. Here's the point Paul was making: Too much of anything controls you. Now flip that around – the Spirit; if we allow Him to fill us, controls us. Being controlled by the Spirit is a good thing. It's what you take in that comes out. It's a revolving cycle. Put in good and good comes out. Put in bad and bad comes out. It's about overflow.

Get on people's nerves

We should be so filled with the Spirit and so in love with Jesus that it gets on other people's nerves. Jesus should jump off of us. Like literally jump off of us and resonate from us. We all know this person. When this person starts talking we know within five minutes where they are in their relationship with Christ. Jesus just resonates from them because they are filled with the Spirit and there's such an overflow. Now, some of us don't really like this person because we think they take this Jesus stuff too serious. Or, could it be that we are jealous of them instead? Just something to think about.

In my personal life I want so much of Jesus that every word I utter will bring Him glory. Does it happen every day all day? Absolutely not. We all have bad days and we all have those times when we are frustrated with life and frustrated with God. But even through our frustration we should still be so filled with the Spirit that He overflows out of our lives. We should get on people's nerves with this Jesus Extra.

"May the God of hope fill you with all joy and peace as you trust in him, so that you may overflow with hope by the power of the Holy Spirit." Romans 15:13

Paul said, "So that you may overflow with hope by the power of the Holy Spirit". When something overflows it has to go somewhere. I'm not very good at physical science and math, but I do understand that a container can only hold so much before the substance being put in it has to release itself to somewhere.

Overflow = "to fill and go beyond", "to the point of flooding"

Think of it like this; let's say you have a 16 ounce cup that is empty and you have a gallon jar that is filled with water. Now it doesn't take a mathematician to know that a 16 ounce cup cannot hold a gallon of water. So this is where the overflow or flooding comes into play. We begin to pour water from the gallon jar into the 16 ounce cup. Once the cup reaches full capacity we continue to pour. The water has to go somewhere, right? Then the cup begins to run over because we have overflowed it with the water from the gallon jar. Water is now going everywhere affecting everything that is close to the 16 ounce cup. That's what God wants to do in our lives through His Holy Spirit. God wants us to be filled so much

Jesus Extra

with His Spirit that He overflows out of our lives and affects everyone that we come in contract with. The Spirit should overflow out of our lives to the point that it gets on people's nerves and they can't help but see Jesus in us.

Time of reflection

* Why is it that Christians are just uncomfortable talking about the work and the person of the Holy Spirit?
* What's the difference between having the Holy Spirit and being filled with the Holy Spirit?
* What is in your closet that you need to move in order for the Spirit to fill that space in your life?
* So what's overflowing out of your life right now? Is it the Spirit of God or is it something you're into that you shouldn't be into? Where's the overflow coming from? What are you filled with?
* Paul said don't be drunk (controlled) with wine. Going deeper with that, whatever is controlling us could be considered wine. So here's a thought to ponder on or discuss: "Don't be controlled by anything other than the Holy Spirit".
* What is controlling you?

Prayer for batteries

Lord, pour Your Spirit on me to the point that Jesus overflows out of my life. Let me not be concerned with what people may think, but only what You think. I want to live a life that glorifies You and that comes only from Your very Spirit. Help me to reorganize my life in order that Your Spirit can penetrate and fill me. Give me the strength to remove the things that I love but that hinders Your work in my life.

Chapter 10
Fight From Where God Told You

How you approach each situation or battle in life will determine the outcome. It doesn't matter how strong you are or how smart you are; your approach will determine whether you win or lose. There's an old saying that we have all probably heard our entire lives; "Pick your battles". I want to add an aspect to that old saying that will (1) give it theological backing, and (2) give you some great advice. "Don't just pick your battles, but pick your battle lines". When you pick your battle lines you determine how the fight is going to be fought. As you pick these battle lines you need to pick them based on your strengths; not your opponent's strengths.

In this chapter we are going to walk through a very familiar story in the Old Testament. I'm sure you've heard this story preached on and taught on since you've been in the nursery. It's the story of David and Goliath. My prayer for you is that when you finish this chapter you will have a whole new outlook on the story and also receive some encouragement through the obstacles that David faced. I say that because every day in life we have battles. I want to encourage you through this that it's how you approach those battles that will determine whether you win or lose, succeed or fail. It's up to you.

"As the Philistine moved closer to attack him, David ran quickly toward the battle line to meet him". 1 Samuel 17:48

You determine where you fight

There's really only one thing in life that scares me. When I say it scares me, I mean I am completely terrified of this one thing. I am scared of snakes. I don't like snakes and will not even be close to a snake. When I go into pet stores I stay away from the area the snakes are in. If you have a pet snake in your home you need counseling. When someone says the word snake I just take off running and ask questions later. No, my fear of snakes has nothing to do with the serpent in the Garden of Eden. I'm just terrified of snakes.

I told you that to tell you this: I had never been turkey hunting before. Well, I was finally talked into going one Spring while I lived in North Arkansas. The guy that took me was even gracious enough to buy me a turkey gun as a present. So we went and I bet we walked four or five miles through the woods that day. We would sit for a while and call turkeys. Some would respond but never get close enough to take a shot at. About ten o'clock that morning we decided to walk back to the truck. For some reason the guy I was with decided to stop one more time and hit his turkey call. So we stopped and I'm standing there while he is attempting to call up a turkey; but with no response. Then he looks right at me and says, "You're standing on a snake". I thought he was messing with me because he knew I was terrified of snakes, so I didn't even look down. Then he said, "Logan, I'm serious. You're standing on a snake". Needless to say, but he wasn't lying. I threw my gun down on the snake and took off running. I don't know where I was running to but it was away from the snake.

I let the snake determine the fight and I ran scared. I had a loaded gun in my hand and all I had to do was slowly aim the gun and kill it. However, I did right the opposite. I actually gave the snake my gun. If we are honest with ourselves we do this all the time. I don't know what the snake is in your life, but you have thrown down your weapon and allowed it to determine where and how you're going to fight. In the story of David and Goliath it's key to understand that David went to the battle line. As believers in the Lord Jesus Christ it's up to us to pick the battle line; not the enemy. The enemy wants to get you in close with his schemes so that he can destroy you. But you have to pick your battle line.

The first part of the story is found in First Samuel chapter seventeen in verses twenty through twenty-seven. In this section of the story David is going to provide his brothers with peanut butter and jelly sandwiches. This section of the story also contains the curses that this large man is spitting out against the Israelites. David's brothers are in King Saul's army and they have been out there in the same spot for forty days listening at this dude named Goliath threaten them every day. David has yet to hear these threats because he's been out in the fields keeping his father's sheep. So when David arrives on the scene where the "battle" is taking place, he is in shock that no one is taking action. In retrospect, there's not much of a battle taking place, just a lot of threatening. You know what I mean; remember being in the third grade and wanting to fight but not want to fight so you and the other person just kind of danced together talking about each other's momma. Well, that's really what's going on here. Everyone wanted to fight but they didn't want to fight.

David had only been out there for a short period of time and all it took was him hearing these threats one time and he was ready for action. Remember; David is just a teenager and probably not even old enough to fight. All these other men have been out there for forty days and everyday Goliath throws out the same exact threat and scares all these grown men. Remember, David who was just a boy, had something that an entire army and a king did not have; a willing spirit.

The king is such a coward that he offers a bounty on Goliath. He offered his daughter to the man who kills Goliath. Not only would this person get the king's daughter in marriage but they would also be exempt from taxes. Now if I'm David, I'm saying, "The no taxes thing sounds like a pretty good deal, but what does the daughter look like?" I'm quite sure that

David heard the story from Genesis where Jacob got conned into marrying Laban's ugly daughter instead of the pretty one. So If I'm David I'm working out the details before I volunteer myself for such a feat.

Battle before the battle before the battle

I want to show you something pretty key in this story. Every time you get ready to do something great, you're going to face opposition. David will actually face two battles before he ever gets to the big showdown with Goliath.

"When Eliab, David's oldest brother, heard him speaking with the men, he burned with anger at him and asked, "Why have you come down here? And with whom did you leave those few sheep in the desert? I know how conceited you are and how wicked your heart is; you came down only to watch the battle"."
1 Samuel 17:28

For starters, how conceited could someone be if all they did was look at sheep all day? I guess I didn't realize that sheep watchers could climb the corporate ladder and wear high dollar suits and driving fancy donkeys.

Let's side track for a moment from David and then we'll come back to this. There's only one time in the entire Bible where the Devil is referred to as the "accuser". In Revelation chapter twelve verse ten the Devil is called the *"accuser of the brethren"*. He comes to us and tells us everything that we can't do. And not only that – he tells us how bad of a person we are. In most cases, we believe it. Now hold that thought for a moment.

Here we see David's own brother accusing him of being conceited and wicked. David went to provide for his brother's needs; and this is the kind of treatment he gets. If I was David I would have smashed his sandwiches and crushed all his potato chips. Well, accusing is exactly what Satan does to us. He says things to us like, "You're not good enough. Look at yourself – you're singing these songs to God after what you did this week. You can't win this battle. You should have stayed in bed today. You know you shouldn't even be here. You're nothing. God doesn't really love you". So you see how it works? He accuses us and makes us feel insignificant. That's his job and he desires to ruin our lives by causing us to get sucked into battles. So many time we believe the accuser when he says things to us.

I hope you see what's happening. That's how Satan draws us in. We tend to forget that we have the power to determine our battle line. We have to determine where we are going to fight from. We may not be able to pick the battle, but it's up to us where the battle is fought from. If you let the enemy determine the battle line you will lose every time.

Unwanted confrontations

Have you ever had to go into a confrontation that you really didn't want to face? You know what I'm talking about. One of those situations that you must handle but you dread it because you know the outcome is not going to be milk and cookies. I had one of these not too long ago. So I made the dreaded phone call to confront someone over a situation that was actually stupid and false. As the conversation continued it began to become heated over the phone. Because I was arguing my point I lost my cool and said some things I shouldn't have to this person (I may be a preacher, but I'm still human). Towards the end of this conversation this person began to just let me have it. They literally chewed me up and spit me out. After getting off the phone I felt completely defeated. I was defeated for several reasons; one, I lost an argument that I was right in and by the end of the conversation I felt like I was in the wrong when in reality I was in the right. And two, I lost it and lost control of how I should have handled it.

I told you that story because I was sucked in by the enemy. The enemy beat me down. I was fighting a fight that had to be fought. My reputation and my integrity was on the line. But in the end I lost because I didn't go to the battle line that God had drawn for me. I got sucked in to the other person's strength. There are going to be times when we get sucked in by the enemy, by the opposition; and when that happens we have to do exactly what David did. I failed to do this in my encounter, but I learned a valuable lesson as I was reading through this story. So check this out.....

> *"He* (David) *then turned away to someone else"* 1 Samuel 17:30

Batteries Not Included

David didn't allow his brother to draw the battle line in their argument. You saw what he did, he just turned away. Now, he could have hung his head, walked back to his donkey, and went back to the sheep allowing his brother to win the battle; but he didn't do that. He turned away and talked to someone more important. When the enemy tries to draw you in, you have got to turn away and talk to someone more important....God. You will never be able to determine your battle line if you don't turn away and go to the battle line that God already has marked.

When was the last time you talked to God before you went into battle? Instead of jumping to conclusions; when did you seek God's advice about how to approach the situation? So many times in our day to day activities we jump to conclusions. I don't understand why, but it is so hard for us to logically think things through when the enemy is attacking us and yelling out threats. We try to go into battle without ever giving God a chance to work out our circumstances. No. It's not fun when someone makes an accusation about us. No. It's not cool when we are trying to do something nice and the other person tells us we are doing it because we are conceited. No. It's not the greatest feeling in the world when someone tells us to go back to those few sheep. So instead of going "beast mode" on someone and losing our cool, we just need to turn away. There's a God that can give us advice and instruction on how to determine when and where to fight. The battle line has been drawn in each of our circumstances, but it's up to us whether or not we cross that line.

Something key we need to understand: just because you turn away doesn't mean that the battle is over. Sometimes the battle will follow you. Always remember, we have to pick our battle lines. Not necessarily the battle because life is full of battles, but we get to pick our battle lines. Even if you have used this concept in the past, just think for a moment about how the battle followed you. You may have even tried to run from a situation only to look behind you and see that it's following you. Even if it's not the same devil or enemy, something will be chasing your heels.

David has already encountered one battle with his brother (whom he went to provide for). Now David is about to have his second battle, but this time it's with the king. Saul catches wind of this shepherd boy's desire to fight for Israel and for God. So as Saul gets this report he inquires of David.

> *"David said to Saul, "Let no one lose heart on account of this Philistine; your servant will go and fight him". Saul replied, "You are not able to go out against this Philistine and fight him; you are only a boy, and he has been a fighting man from his youth"."* 1 Samuel 17:32-33

David encounters his second battle and he's yet to face the giant. Luckily they are just verbal encounters and not physical altercations. However, David tells the king, "your entire army is scared of this guy, but I will go out and fight him". So then what did Saul do? He tried to determine David's battle line by telling him that he was not qualified. "Who are you, you are just a boy, all you do is watch sheep, this giant will destroy you, just because you can play a harp really well that doesn't mean jack, this dude will mess up your pretty face". However, David didn't get sucked into the king's trap because David knew that God had already given him the victory because he knew where his battle line was.

Here's some piercing questions for you: Do you know where your battle line is? Do you even understand what the battle line is or represents. The battle line in the heat of battle is the most important thing in your life at that moment (a part from God). Don't get sucked into the enemy's schemes. If you get sucked in you can't blame your circumstances on God. It's our own human reasoning that tells us to push it to the limit.

I can remember as a kid that my mother would tell me how far up the street in the neighborhood I could go. I always pushed the issue and stretched her rope that she was giving me. When I thought she was busy in the house I would go a little farther than I was told. Then as I got comfortable I would push that line even farther out there. I'm quite sure you've done the same thing as a child so quit thinking to yourself about how rebellious I was. However in everyday life and especially in the heat of daily battles we tend to do this same thing with the battles lines that God has drawn for us. If only we could understand that God placed those lines there for a reason.

Remember, your battle lines determine how and where you fight. Don't get sucked in. I'm pleading with you to not get sucked in. Right now though, maybe you've already been sucked in and maybe you've even turned away. It's like you can't get away from it no matter what you do. I know. I'm with you. As we walk through the rest of this story my prayer is that you can find hope in your circumstances.

Live to fight another day

I can't emphasize enough that David is in the middle of his second battle and he hasn't even made it to Goliath yet. He's already had a verbal dispute with his brother and now he is in one with the king. David didn't get sucked into the king's trap because he knew that God had already given him the victory because he knew where his battle line was. So look at David's response to the king; which is also his reasoning why he is not scared and the fact that God is with him.

"But David said to Saul, "Your servant has been keeping his father's sheep. When a lion or a bear came and carried off a sheep from the flock, I went after it, struck it and rescued the sheep from its mouth. When it turned on me, I seized it by its hair, struck it and killed it. Your servant has killed both the lion and the bear; this uncircumcised Philistine will be like one of them, because he has defied the armies of the living God. The Lord who delivered me from the paw of the lion and the paw of the bear will deliver me from the hand of this Philistine"." 1 Samuel 17:34-37a

What David's brother did not know and what the king did not know was that God had been training David for this very moment. I don't know what you're going through right now, But I can promise you that God is training you to have a major victory in your life. You just need to listen to God and let Him determine your battle line. Listen to me when I tell you this: the battle line is the most important part of the battle because if you get sucked in, you will lose every time.

How many lions and bears have you chased in your life? You may be thinking, *none*. Well, in a literal sense, no me either. As a matter of fact, I'm not going to chase any animal that can kill me. But in a spiritual sense we have all chased these things. It may be something God told you to do and you went after it. Yes, you were scared of the outcome but God gave you the victory. That's what David was trying to get across to this self-centered king. God used David's past circumstances to prepare him for this very moment. What is God preparing you for? You may not see it right now because you're in the heat of a battle, but you have been trained this very moment. Get ready because God is going to do something big in your life if you fight from where He told you.

Yeah right

At the end of verse 37 Saul gave David one of the most ridiculous responses. What he said was not ridiculous, but how he said it is what made it ridiculous. Now, none of us were there during the conversation between David and King Saul; but just going off the arrogant attitude that scripture clearly gives us regarding Saul, I honestly feel it's safe to make the assumption that when Saul said to David, "and the Lord be with you"…..what he was really saying was "yeah right! Little dude, you are about to die and this will last about as long as it took for Mike Tyson to knock out Marvis Frazier (thirty seconds if you were wondering)". Then on top of that, the king tries to publically humiliate David by putting armor on David that he picked up from the Big and Tall section of the armor store. David keeps his cool and politely tells the king that he will just take a sling and a stone with him into battle. Goliath has a sword and is wearing armor and David has on no protection and nothing to fight hand to hand combat with.

Don't you love it when the odds are against you? I know what you're thinking, "Not really". Don't you love it when those who are supposed to support you don't give you a chance? Again, I know what you're thinking; "Not really". I understand. No one in their right frame of mind goes up against a giant who is completely covered in armor and is carrying a sword that weighs more than you do. No one does this except for God. Guess what? God is out of your mind. We cannot comprehend the things He does and why He chooses to do them. But God loves it when the odds are against Him and no one gives Him a chance. This gives Him the opportunity to show off His power in my life and in your life…..and in this shepherd boy's life.

Batteries Not Included

In the story it emphasizes that as David goes out to fight Goliath that Goliath kept trying to come closer to David. Goliath even taunts David with a good tongue lashing (I'm sure David was thinking to himself, "I've been beaten up verbally twice already, what's one more time?). Goliath needs David to get close so that he can either get his hands on David or be able to swing his sword. This is emphasized in the story in verses forty-one and forty-four when it says, Goliath kept coming closer to David and even said to David, *"come here and I'll destroy you"*. You know what? Goliath was absolutely right. If David had allowed himself to be lured in he would have instantly been killed by the giant. If Goliath would have gotten his hands on this little boy; he would have crushed his skull with just his bare hands. David knew it.

The reason many Christians lose battles in life is because they allow themselves to get too close to the enemy. Whatever the situation is; we always seem to get into arm's reach of it and the next thing you know we are beaten down and then we start to doubt everything God has told us. So it's our fault for allowing ourselves to get too close to the enemy. When the enemy grabs us he can hurt us. Please learn this basic principle from David. This is not just a children's story that we learn in children's church, this is real life and the situations you face in life are real and they are against real giants. The giants and the doubters are looking at you and they're saying, "Yeah Right!" It's up to you to prove them wrong by fighting from where God told you.

Fight From Where God Told You

If David would have fought the battle on Goliath's terms he would have lost; Even if he was fighting for the right reason. Some of us today are fighting battles for the right reason, but we're still losing because we're fighting on the enemy's terms. We didn't go to the battle line; therefore we are losing the battle. We crossed over the line into enemy territory and that's why many of us are just being beaten down by our circumstances. You can really love God and still be losing in life because you crossed over the battle line.

As Goliath got closer to David, look at what David did. *"As the Philistine moved closer to attack him, David ran quickly toward the battle line to meet him"* (verse forty-eight). Where did David run to? The battle line, to where God told him to fight from. David did not run because he was scared of Goliath. If David was scared he would have went back to watching the sheep after he and his brother had that argument. David ran because his strength was at the battle line, not hand to hand combat. Do you understand where your strength is? The situation you are facing right now; are you being beaten down because you're fighting on the enemies terms?

Goliath tried to determine how the battle was going to be fought. Here's the beautiful thing about David running to the battle line and how we need to run to the battle line when we are faced with a situation in life: The enemy can't kill you as long as you don't get close. The situation that you are facing in life right now will not hurt you if you run to the battle line. Don't get lured into arm's reach. Run to the battle line and use the weapons that God has given you. If you want victory in your life and in your circumstances, you got to run to the battle line.

But here's the deal: Just because you make it to the battle line safely doesn't mean that it's over. It's called a "battle line" for a reason. You've got to get out your sling and your stones and kill every giant that's in your way. You have to sling those stones at every negative situation in your life. Don't get sucked in. You will not win if you do. Use the weapons that God gave you and use them from the battle line.

The victory is yours

David did not fight the battle on Goliath's terms. He fought the battle on his own terms because he understood how important it was to make it to the battle line. Do you realize how important your battle line is today? It's not that we pick our battles; it's that we pick our battle lines. That's what will determine whether or not you live in victory or live in defeat. David is about to accomplish something so great that it will completely change the trajectory of his life and the trajectory of a kingdom.

> *"Reaching into his bag and taking out a stone, he slung it and struck the Philistine on the forehead. The stone sank into his forehead, and he fell facedown on the ground. So David triumphed over the Philistine with a sling and a stone; without a sword in his hand he struck down the Philistine and killed him".* 1 Samuel 17:49-50

Fight From Where God Told You

In life we've got to learn how to draw our battle lines and say "I'm fighting from right here". As God's people it's up to us to determine how and where we fight the good fight of faith. Don't give into the Devil's schemes. You fight from the battle lines that God has provided for you. If you do that you will win every time. God wants us to live a full life....a life that is victorious every day. Yes there will be days when we are down in the dumps and we question all the promises of God; but those days are not what should define us. God has equipped us with the proper weapons to take on all our enemies; especially the Devil.

The enemy may draw a sword on you and it may be a big sword and it will probably scare you; but if you don't get close enough to the enemy his sword will be useless. Paper beats rock, rock beats scissors, scissors beat paper. Never the less, a sling and stone from your battle line will always beat the sword of the enemy. So when the giant in your life comes at you; what are you going to do? Are you going to let your situation lure you in? Or are you going to run to your battle line and handle your business. So after you handle your business there's one more thing you have to do......you have to finish the job!!! This is where it gets good.

"David ran and stood over him. He took hold of the Philistine's sword and drew it from the scabbard. After he killed him, he cut off his head with the sword. When the Philistines saw that their hero was dead, they turned and ran". 1 Samuel 17:51

Not only did David kill the enemy, but it scared the rest of the Philistine army so bad that they ran. So the next time Satan or any other enemy tries to lure you in through a negative situation, you run to your battle line – handle your business – then go cut off his head – then just sit back and watch what the power of Jesus can do in your life because the demons will flee. It's because you bare the name of Christ that gives you power over every situation in your life. The Israelite army said that Goliath was too big to fight. But David said that Goliath was too big to miss. Draw your battle line and watch what God can do through your life.

Living victorious through circumstances is up to how you approach each and every situation you encounter. The victory is yours. Now go get it!

Time of Reflection

* Looking back at some of the battles (situations) in your life; how have you taken the wrong approach in some of those?
* Why is it so important to fight life from the place God told us to fight?
* Think about your current circumstances right now…or maybe something you just recently went through; how has or is God training you for your next encounter?
* Have you been sucked in and hurt before? What did that feel like? I'm sure not very pleasant. But what did you learn from that experience?

* Why do you think Christians live defeated lives?
* Think about the weapons that God has equipped you with. No not literal weapons, but weapons within our personalities. Examples: think things through, strong willed, intellect, visionary, prayer warrior, etc. How can you use your weapons to your advantage?
* Still thinking about your weapons; what can the enemy do to you when you fail to utilize the weapons God has given you?
* Make a commitment to not get lured in and to always fight from where God told you to fight.

Prayer for Batteries

Lord, lay out the lines in which I must take on life. There are circumstances that look like giants to me. There are battles before the battles. Give me the proper weapons and gifts that I can use to ensure victory in life. No man, no giant, and no army is too much for You. My strength lies in You God. So guard me from getting sucked in by the opposition and to fight from where You told me. Thank You in advance for the victories You're going to give me.

Chapter 11

Winning the War

❦

When I was in the ninth grade we had a bigger kid that was a bully. He never picked on me but he did pick on kids that were smaller than he was. One day he decided to call me out in class. We were sitting in Health class and he sat beside me and he said fairly loudly, "Ferguson, after school I'm going to get you". Well, several scenarios played through my mind rather quickly. We did ride the same bus and he did live in my neighborhood, which meant we would have to get off the bus together. Then something inside of me kind of went haywire. So I answered back quickly and loudly with, "Why wait"? It was then that I reached across the aisle and punched him right in the eye. He fell out of his desk onto the floor. Of course the entire class erupted. There wasn't much of a fight. Just two hits. I hit him and he hit the floor. What's funny about this, I didn't even get in trouble, he did. The coach that was teaching the Health class heard him threaten me.

Winning the War

In life sometimes you have to take circumstances for what they are. Now I'm not telling you to go around punching people; but I am telling you to not put up with nonsense. Sometimes it's pretty plain what we need to do and the direction we need to go. I'm not an advocate of fighting and randomly punching people, but I am one hundred percent against bullying. If kids would start defending themselves there would be less bullying. I'm not telling you to get into a fight, but if you are forced to defend yourself…..then let the chips fall where they may.

We are going to look at a guy named Gideon. He's not much to look at and doesn't have much. He even admits that his clan/family is the least of them all. He knows he isn't much. He knows that the Israelites have been picked on. He even questions God's integrity by picking him to save Israel. However, God chose him to do some amazing things.

"When the angel of the LORD appeared to Gideon, he said, "The LORD is with you, mighty warrior." "But sir", Gideon replied, "if the LORD is with us, why has all this happened to us? Where are all his wonders that our fathers told us about when they said, 'Did not the LORD bring us up out of Egypt?' But now the LORD has abandoned us and put us into the hand of Midian." The LORD turned to him and said, "Go in the strength you have and save Israel out of Midian's hand. Am I not sending you?"" Judges 6:12-14

Batteries Not Included

You want to know what God is saying? Quit sitting around whining about your circumstances and do something about it. Gideon was in hiding. Have you ever been in hiding or denial about a situation you were going through? You completely shut the world out of your life? You know what I'm talking about. You wallowing in your filth and having a pity party. We've all been there and done that. If you haven't.... just hang on because it's coming. Let me give you a nickel's worth of advice that will spend like fifty dollars: the only person that can change what you're going through.... is you.

Let me talk about this bully again: If I had let this dude get the best of me he could have caused me to live in fear. This knucklehead could have ruined my life. So instead of living in fear I stood up for myself and every other kid he bullied; and was the hero to everyone in the ninth grade. You want to know something fascinating? He didn't bully anyone else. When Gideon decided to do something about his situation – God did some amazing stuff through him. His name literally means, "mighty warrior". How cool is that?

When God tells you to do something crazy

What we are about to talk about is the story where God defied all the odds. If this thing was in Vegas it would be a sure enough hands down winner for those fighting against God. Looking at the odds, God is definitely going to lose this time. The beautiful thing about God; He is God. His resources are unlimited and His power can't be matched. There are times when God will not intervene in our situation until it becomes humanly impossible. God loves it when the odds are against Him and His children.

Maybe God is asking you to go against the odds. Maybe God is asking you and us as a church to go against everything that seems "churchy". God may be asking you to step out of your comfort zone so that you can really do something great for Him. What is God inviting you to do that you should already be doing? Whatever it is; God has got your back. Let me tell you this: When you step out and do what God has told you to do, it's not your reputation on the line – it's God's reputation on the line. God is not going to let His reputation be ruined.

> *"Early in the morning, Jerub-Baal (that is, Gideon) and all his men camped at the spring of Harod. The camp of Midian was north of them in the valley near the hill of Moreh. The LORD said to Gideon, "You have too many men for me to deliver Midian into their hands. In order that Israel may not boast against me that her own strength has saved her, announce now to the people, 'Anyone who trembles with fear may turn back and leave Mount Gilead.'" So twenty-two thousand men left, while ten thousand remained."* Judges 7:1-3

For starters, Gideon had thirty-two thousand men ready for war. But this is what I want you to know; they were already vastly outnumbered. The story tells us in verse twelve that the other army had so many that the people were thick as locusts and their camels couldn't be counted. So thirty-two thousand against an army that is so numerous they couldn't be counted; yeah I'd say the odds are definitely against Gideon, Israel, and God. What's so crazy about God sometimes is that although they were already outnumbered and the odds were stacked against them, God said, "that's too many men in your army". God likes it when the odds are against Him. Why? Because if we do it on our own strength and resources we get the glory and we leave God out. God wants all the glory all the time. That's why God told Gideon, "You have too many men in your army or they will boast about the victory".

If I'm Gideon I'm trying to work out a compromise with the Lord. Don't start acting all spiritual because you know you would do the same thing. God will not compromise when His reputation and His glory is on the line. Not only did God say there were too many men once; but He said it twice. Twenty-two thousand have already bailed because they were scared. We only started out with thirty-two thousand. Now we're down to ten thousand. The other armies have too many to even number. But God said, "Nope. That's still too many".

If Gideon had attacked with the full thirty-two thousand and won I'm sure the Israelites would have graciously thanked God for His guidance and battle plan, but God still wouldn't have received full credit. God wants and deserves full credit for the victories in our life. That's why He waits until we run out of resources to intervene in our situations. That's why He waits until you are completely broke before He provides you with a financial breakthrough. That's why He waits until you are at the bottom of the barrel before He delivers you. That's why He waits until nothing goes our way before He intervenes. He wants all the glory because it's His reputation on the line, not yours.

At the exact moment when Gideon thought it couldn't get any worse number wise; check this out……

> *"But the LORD said to Gideon, "There are still too many men. Take then down to the water, and I will sift through them for you there. If I say, 'this one shall go with you', he shall go; but if I say, 'This one shall not go with you,' he shall not go".* Judges 7:4

The style in which God uses to pick Gideon's army is actually comical. The remaining ten thousand men go to the water to get a drink. God knew they were thirsty. This is what's so funny about this story. Some of the men made a cup out of their hands and drank with dignity while others got down on all fours and drank like dogs. The scripture says that they literally *lapped water with their tongues like a dog.* Ok, so let's be real here, if I see you drinking water like a dog, I don't want you fighting in my army either. Now here's what stinks about all of this; ten thousand of them went to get a drink of water and out of that number nine thousand and seven hundred grown men acted like they didn't have any manners. I'm not a mathematician, and I don't want to come across as rude or mean, but ninety-seven percent of what was left in this army were evidently lacking the mental capacity to be able to fight in an army. Needless to say, but God didn't have to draw straws on who he sifted out for Gideon.

Seriously God?

Have you ever asked someone a question in the form of a statement? Have you ever said, "Seriously God"? Yeah that's right. "Seriously God". It's ok because we've all said that to God before. The text doesn't imply that Gideon said that, but he was human and he already admitted he wasn't much, so I'm sure he at least thought it. There are times in our lives when God does addition by subtraction. It's crazy to comprehend why and what God does sometimes, but this is where our faith is elevated to the next level. It's either elevated or we run from God. Just a reminder, the last guy that literally ran from God was swallowed by a literal fish. So be careful when you say "Really God". Gideon may or may not have said that, but he did just go from thirty-two thousand to ten thousand. Then we go from ten thousand to three hundred. OK God – the other army is too numerous to even count.

Here comes another "Seriously God" moment. After this major addition by subtraction thing that only works when God is doing the math; God does something even more ridiculous that will make the odds even worse for the Israelites. Before we get to that I want you to understand this: Maybe our impossible situations are opportunities for God to do something

Winning the War

miraculous in our lives because we will have no other option but to give Him the glory. Just when we think we can't go on, God stretches us a little farther…..

"Dividing the three hundred men into three companies, he placed trumpets and empty jars in the hands of all of them, with torches inside". Judges 7:16

They were told to hold a trumpet in one hand and an empty jar in the other. The empty jar was their torch. Somehow an empty jar had a torch in it. I don't understand it, but that's just what the Bible says. The things God does sometimes! Now; I'm not the smartest man in the world and have never even claimed to be smart. As a matter of fact, for those who know me personally, they'd be the first to say, "Yeah, he's not too smart". But, it doesn't take a rocket scientist to figure this out……If they had a trumpet in one hand and a jar in the other….what were they going to hold their swords with? If I'm in this undersized army I'm thinking; what does God want us to fight with, a sound and light show? The answer is "yes". They didn't even need their swords because God is the sword.

The men were then divided up into three different sections. So that's one hundred men in each section. (That's about the extent of my math skills). They have their jars and they have their trumpets and they are prepared to display a Fourth of July show before the Fourth of July existed. This is so cool……

"The three companies blew the trumpets and smashed the jars. Grasping the torches in their left hands and holding in their right hands the trumpets they were to blow, they shouted, "A sword for the LORD and for Gideon!" While each man held his position around the camp, all the Midianites ran, crying out as they fled. When the three hundred trumpets sounded, the LORD caused the men throughout the camp to turn on each other with their swords" Judges 7:20-22a

God loves it when the odds are against Him because He always gets the glory. Most of our problems in life aren't necessarily our current circumstances; but how we view our circumstances. It's the perception of our circumstances. What we see as a massive army or a huge situation we are facing, God sees it as an opportunity to defy the odds that are against us. What we see as big, God sees as small. That's how you win the war. You win the war by seeing things in life the way that God sees things in life. There is no army too big or too strong for our God. There is no problem in your life that you can't overcome when you rely on God's guidance and God's strength.

If God can take a man, who admittedly said he and his family were the least of them all, save an entire nation, then what can God do with you and through you? You take on life with your strategy and you will lose. You take on life with God's strategy (even as ridiculous as it may seem) you will be victorious every single time. You want to win the war in life.... then do it God's way and not your.

One of the greatest pieces of advice I'd ever received I have to credit it to my dad. I was struggling through some personal issues and I was leaving God completely out. I'm going to end this chapter with the exact words my dad said to. It was simply this, "You tried it your way and it didn't work. Why don't you try it God's way"?

Time of Reflection

* Has God been telling you to do something that you've been putting off because you're relying on your own strength instead of God's?
* Think about this: Greatness doesn't happen until you decide to do something. What do you think about this statement?
* How many times in your life have you taken the glory for something God clearly did?
* Why do we as humans tend to have the "look at me" attitude?
* As you think back about the odds that God overcame through Gideon and only 300 men, what are you up against right now that appears you may lose to?
* Why does God wait until we are completely out of human resources before He intervenes?
* What is God wanting to do through you? And why are you scared to "go for it"?

Prayer for Batteries

Lord, I can't face this battle on my own; but through You I can face anything. God, even if it takes removing my resources for me to depend on You fully, have Your way Lord. Let me never take credit for the victories You have provided. Lord, I need Your guidance and Your strategy. No matter what battle comes next, when the victory is won, everyone will know that You are God.

Chapter 12
Finish Strong

Would you say that right now in your life you're where you want to be or need to be? What is it that you need to move on from in order to finish strong? Maybe you're just beaten completely down right now. You want to bounce back and finish strong but you don't know how. Maybe you've done some things and you're thinking to yourself, "It's just best if I give up". Or maybe you're thinking, "My life is so jacked up that God won't forgive me".

Let me tell you this: There's hope! As long as you're still breathing there's hope. Eric Thomas, known as the "Hip Hop Preacher" is quoted as saying, "If you can look up, you can get up".[5] Feeding off what Pastor Thomas said, there's hope for you. It doesn't matter what your life has become or the choices you've made up to this point in life, if you're breathing and reading this book you can finish strong.

---

[5] Thomas, Eric. Pastor and Author. Hip Hop Preacher

We are going to look at a guy who completely ruined his life. What he did with his life is beyond anything that we could grasp. So if this guy can find hope and peace, then so can you.

Before we get to this other guy, let's get personal for a few minutes. Think about this: How do you want people to remember you? What do you want to be known for? Let's put this in the context of sports because just about everyone loves some type of sport. In sports you have a winner and a loser. It's either/or…no in between. Ties don't count because neither person or team wins. No tie goes down as the greatest event. However, your team can be getting dominated for most of the game; but if for some reason your team comes back and wins – you know – finishes strong, you don't remember how badly they played, all you remember is that they fought back and won. Now in terms of life; maybe you're struggling in this fight right now and it looks like you're definitely going to lose and be beaten down. To change that all you need is a little momentum shift. When the momentum starts going your way you can finish strong. Life is about momentum. Momentum is something in motion. Life is momentum in motion.

The downhill slide

The downhill slide is always the most dangerous direction to go in life. Things go haywire and completely get out of control. The next thing you know, much of life has slipped you by. One decision leads to another decision which leads to another decision. You get the picture, it's a downhill slide.

> *"Manasseh was twelve years old when he became king, and he reigned in Jerusalem fifty-five years. He did evil in the eyes of the Lord, following the detestable practices of the nations the LORD had driven out before the Israelites"*. 2 Chronicles 33:1-2

The first problem we see is that he was twelve years old and running a country. No twelve year old should ever have this type of responsibility on their shoulders. They are set up for failure. Manasseh was destined to fail. For you Bible gurus, yes I know that Manasseh's grandson Josiah was eight years old when he took the throne. But it wasn't until he was about sixteen years old that he began to seek the Lord. Either way, a kid shouldn't be running a country. Both had influencers they looked to. So maybe, just maybe, Josiah's circle of influence was spiritually better than Manasseh's. Your influencers make an impact on your life. That's why I focused an entire chapter on influence.

We know that Manasseh had some knowledge about the Lord and we know that he knew what he was "supposed to do". His father was Hezekiah, whom the Bible called one of the greatest kings to ever live because God was with him.

> *"Hezekiah trusted in the LORD, the God of Israel. There was no one like him among all the kings of Judah, either before him or after*

him. He held fast to the Lord and did not cease to follow him; he kept the commands the LORD had given Moses. And the LORD was with him; he was successful in whatever he undertook." 2 Kings 18:5-7a

Being in this type of environment (which we would call a Christian home) you would think that Manasseh would have just followed in his father's footsteps and kept everything flowing the Jesus way. Unfortunately it's up to us to make our own choices in life. God did not create us as robots. So because we are allowed to make our own choices – sometimes in life we make them and it starts us on the downhill slide; or you could say slippery slope.

A slippery slope is a logical fallacy that means when you step in one direction that another will follow and then another until you're headed full steam in that direction in life. Your momentum has you going in one direction. This can be either positive or negative. You get to choose. Once that slippery slope gathers up enough momentum it's hard to stop, much less reverse. That's why it's so critical that we think through the choices we make in life. What's so bad about this slippery slope full of momentum is that once we are on it, it's so easy to take others with us…..again, it still involves influence.

"But Manasseh led Judah and the people of Jerusalem astray, so that they did more evil than the nations the LORD had destroyed before the Israelites". 2 Chronicles 33:9

Manasseh made some poor choices and it not only took him down a slippery slope personally, but it led a nation into the gutter as well. Our choices in life not only affect us, but they affect our circle of influence as well. Next thing you know....things get completely out of control. Then at that point when you think things couldn't get any worse and you think that Manasseh couldn't become any more evil....check out what he does.........

"He sacrificed his sons in the fire in the Valley of Ben Hinnom, practiced sorcery, divination and witchcraft, and consulted mediums and spiritists. He did much evil in the eyes of the LORD, provoking him to anger". 2 Chronicles 33:6

This dude was so far from the Lord that he started killing his kids as a form of worshipping a false god. This guy didn't just have a cussing problem, his problem wasn't his anger or road rage, he didn't have an alcohol problem; he was killing his own children!!! Now I know that we can all stray from the Lord, but surely not to the point where we start sacrificing our children. None of us have ever done anything that bad; but that voice in our head has told us that we have....and we believe it. Our minds take us into captivity and we feel trapped in our sins. Once our mind takes us captive we will do some crazy things that are out of touch with reality.

When we get out of touch with reality we are out of touch with God and we can't even hear Him when

Batteries Not Included

He speaks to us. Often times in life we are so consumed by our circumstances that we don't hear God the first time He speaks to us. The story tells us that God spoke to Manasseh and the people, but they did not listen. The text actually says in verse ten that, *"they paid no attention"*.

I've read this story numerous times, but for some reason that verse really jumped out at me when I was working on a sermon one day. It raised several questions in my mind that actually haunted me. Think about this: Have you ever become so arrogant in your life and even in your sin that you thought you were invincible? I know I have. I admit that I have. Sometimes we get so trapped that we begin to do things that we swore we'd never do. There's an old saying that says, "Never say never". Boy isn't that is so true? Often times when we have veered off this road that God has us on we began to compromise with ourselves and do things that we said, "We'd never do". We not only lose touch with reality but we lose touch with God and His voice. It is because God loves us so much that He jars our life and our circumstances because we would not listen to Him. He has to do something drastic to get our attention.

> *"So the LORD brought against them the army commanders of the king of Assyria, who took Manasseh prisoner, put a hook in his nose, bound him with bronze shackles and took him to Babylon."* 2 Chronicles 33:11

That's a heck of a nose ring right there. I don't have my nose pierced, but if I was to get it done I'm not going to the Assyrian Tattoo and Piercing Parlor in downtown Babylon. Sometimes God has to really do something life altering to get our attention. I wish I knew why we didn't listen to God better. I wish I had the answers for why God's children stray from Him. I wish I could provide every parent with encouragement from the Proverbs twenty-two verse six that says, *"Train up a child in the way he should go, and when he is old he will not depart from it"* (King James Version). I believe that the fear every Christian parent has is that their children will stray from the Lord and do things that they swore they would never do. I also believe that the All-Knowing and Sovereign God is utterly heart-broken when this happens. He is heart-broken for the parents as well as the one who went astray. Even though the situation is bad there is hope because it's through captivity that we begin to call out to God.

The uphill climb

The rest of the story of Manasseh, particularly verses 12 and 13 are proof that there's absolutely nothing that you can do that will make God forget about you and not love you. This dude was way out there….like over the fence. He wasn't just hanging out in left field; he had completely climbed over the fence and was heading into never-never land. Even through that God still loved Manasseh and He opened His ears to Manasseh's prayers even though Manasseh did not previously listen to God. Maybe that's where you're at right now? God has spoken to you but you've ignored Him and now it's time to call out to God in your distress. Are you in distress right now? Do you need to finish strong in life? Then start your uphill climb by calling out to God.

"In his distress he sought the favor of the LORD his God and humbled himself greatly before the God of his fathers. And when he prayed to him, the LORD was moved by his entreaty and listened to his plea; so he brought him back to Jerusalem and to his kingdom. Then Manasseh knew that the LORD is God". 2 Chronicles 33:12-13

It doesn't matter what you've done or how far you've strayed from God because He wants you back. God wants you back. You are a product of the God who created everything. You are His greatest creation and He wants you back. You have to finish strong. God brought Manasseh back because he wanted to finish strong. Do you want to finish strong? God wants you to but you've got to want it. You've got to go at it life like it depends on God…..because it does. Finish strong.

God's plans for you are bigger than you could ever image and He doesn't want you throwing your life away. He loves you too much to see you do that. But you've got to call out to Him in your distress. I'm pleading with you to humble yourself as Manasseh did and call out to the God of Heaven. Don't worry about what others will think of you. Don't worry about what you may have to leave behind. Don't worry if you have to end a relationship to get back to God. God will work out all the details in your life and in your circumstances.

When you decide to get serious with God and call out to Him, something beautiful is going to happen in your life. No, I can't promise you a care free life because I would be telling you the most unbiblical thing ever. However, I can tell you that the batteries you need are in God's hands. Not only did God bring Manasseh back, but God completely restored him. God gave him everything that he had before. This time though Manasseh knew the Lord. Manasseh had God in his life.

Where do you want to be in life? What is it that you need to move from? You've got to go through the valley to get to the mountain top. Start the uphill climb today. Get your momentum going in the direction that God wants to take you. Finish Strong.

Time of Reflection

* Where ARE you at right now, really? Be honest with yourself and do an honest evaluation deep inside your heart.
* When you're lying in that casket one day, how do you want to be remembered? What do you want to be known for?
* The "Slippery Slope" can be a dangerous thing and can cause our life to spin out of control. What can you do to NOT find yourself on the slippery slope that takes you downhill?

* What is it that leads us to the point of doing things that we "swore we'd NEVER do"?
* Looking back over some circumstances; how has your mind taken you captivity?
* Why are we as Christians, so hard headed.... to the point we can't hear God when He speaks to us?
* Would you say that momentum is the key to going in the right direction?
* What steps do you need to take right now in order to get your momentum going on the uphill climb?
* Decide today, right now to get serious with God and call out to Him. Finish Strong!!!

Prayer for Batteries

Lord, you are the creator of life and the scientific genius behind momentum. Let me take the proper steps to ensure that my momentum goes in Your direction and not a slippery slope that leads me on a path away from You. Yes Lord, I have had many failures, but You love me too much to leave me out there. Thank You for calling out to me and thank You for hearing my call back. I will finish strong and it's by Your strength that it will happen. Thank You, Thank You, Thank You!!!

Chapter 13
There's Hope

Life is crazy sometimes. There will be days when you go into it ready to conquer the world. Then there are days when you don't even want to get out of the bed. On those days there's not enough caffeine to get you started. It's through the ups and downs of life that shape us and mold us into the person that God desires us to be. Because this life moves so fast we have to cherish every opportunity and take advantage of every day. The great theologian Ferris Bueller said, "Life moves pretty fast. If you don't stop and look around once in a while you could miss it".[6] That is so true. We tend to get trapped in the hustle and bustle of life and we get so caught up in ourselves and our problems that we completely miss life. We completely miss out on the opportunities that God has laid out before us.

---

[6] Bueller, Ferris. Ferris Bueller's Day Off. Movie. 1986.

One of these days we will be sitting in a rocking chair, looking out into nowhere wondering what happened. Wondering where God was. Wondering "what if" we had lived our life for God and used the batteries that He had given us numerous times. I can personally tell you that I refuse to live an unlived life. I've missed out on so many opportunities that God has given me that I refuse to miss another one. I want all God all the time. I want God's batteries because that's where His unlimited power source comes from.

Don't miss another opportunity that God gives you. You need batteries and God has an unlimited supply. It doesn't matter what others think about you, it doesn't matter how shaken your faith is, it doesn't matter what adverse situation life throws at you, because you have the Spirit of God living in you and you have already been battle tested so finish this thing strong. Go to God and get your batteries.

Prayer for Batteries

Lord, give me Your endless supply of batteries.
Let Your power never leave my side.

About the Author

Logan Ferguson is the Student Minister at First Baptist Church in Danville, Arkansas. He has served several churches in Arkansas as both Pastor and Youth Pastor. Logan has spoken at numerous events, revivals, led camps, and weekend retreats. He speaks in numerous churches each year as he shares hope for those who are struggling in faith and life. He has a unique style of bringing the scriptures out in a way that is relevant to today's society. His approach is very down to earth and clear, but also challenging to those of all walks of life. It doesn't matter whether you are a new Christian, old Christian, or have never met the Lord personally; Logan has a way of engaging everyone. He has a heart for people and desires for everyone to deepen their walk with God. Logan holds a B.A. in the Bible with a Minor in History from Central Baptist College in Conway, AR.

Logan's hobbies include family time (first and foremost), golf, hunting, fishing, reading, and trying to master the art of wood working. You can follow Logan on Facebook, Twitter @RevLFerg, Instagram revlferg. Logan uses social media as an avenue to provide people encouragement. Logan is even on Pinterest. To book a speaking engagement or enquire about copies of the book you can personally reach Logan through email at <u>revlferg@yahoo.com</u>

Endnotes

[1] Webster's Dictionary & Thesaurus. Identity. Polskabook. Poland. 2006. 185.

[2] Evan, Tony. Tony Evan's Book of Illustrations. Moody Publishers. Chicago. 2009. 141.

[3] Webster's Dictionary & Thesaurus. Surrender. Polskabook. Poland. 2006. 381.

[4] Webster's Dictionary & Thesaurus. Influence. Polskabook. Poland. 2006. 193.

[5] Thomas, Eric. Pastor and Author. Hip Hop Preacher.

[6] Bueller, Ferris. Ferris Bueller's Day Off. Movie. 1986.

CPSIA information can be obtained at www.ICGtesting.com
Printed in the USA
LVOW10s0432290515

440331LV00001B/23/P